PHYSICIANS' UNTOLD STORIES

PHYSICIANS' UNTOLD STORIES

MIRACULOUS EXPERIENCES DOCTORS ARE HESITANT TO SHARE WITH THEIR PATIENTS, OR ANYONE!

~

Scott J. Kolbaba, MD

ISBN-13: 9781530841578
ISBN-10: 1530841577
Library of Congress Control Number: 2016905472
CreateSpace Independent Publishing Platform
North Charleston, South Carolina

This book is dedicated to the loves of my life:
my wife, Joan;
my children, Bethany, Dane, Nathan, Ian, Jordan, Florin,
and Luciana;
their respective spouses, Todd, Leilani, Mandy, and Jessica;
and my grandchildren, Danika, Zoey, Cameron, Elyssa, Quinn,
Wyatt, Grayden, Avery, and Olivia.
They are what it's all about.

CONTENTS

INTRODUCTION

~

"MR. KOLBABA, I'M SORRY TO tell you that you just don't have what it takes to become a doctor. You should give up your ideas and get a regular job."

This was the concluding comment from one of the most powerful physicians in Chicago medicine, the dean of a prestigious Chicago medical school, during my medical school interview in 1971.

I was devastated. I simply could not imagine being anything but a doctor, and it took me several weeks to get over his "advice." True, I was not the most studious college student, but his statement, instead of demoralizing me, motivated me. I was now a student on fire. *Nothing* would keep me from my goal of getting into medical school and becoming the absolute best doctor I could be.

As a recent graduate of Cornell College, I was working full-time, but I enrolled at Roosevelt University in the only evening organic chemistry course in the Chicago area, because I had missed this course as an undergraduate. The commute from my home in DeKalb was nearly seventy miles each way, so I would prop my book up on the steering wheel and memorize the formulas (I would not advise that today).

In my "leisure" time, I studied all the basic subjects that comprised the Medical College Admission Test (MCAT).

The next year when I took the MCAT, my scores improved from the twentieth percentile to over the ninetieth percentile, and two medical schools offered me places in their entering classes. My motivation continued, and I graduated with honors from the University of Illinois College of Medicine. For my residency, I chose the nearby school that had advised me to give up my medical aspirations. In a rare stroke of poetic justice, the faculty there voted me Intern of the Year, an award presented by the same dean's office that had initially advised me to give up!

I transferred again to complete my residency in internal medicine at the Mayo Clinic in Rochester, Minnesota. I subsequently entered private practice in Wheaton, Illinois, and have loved every minute of my thirty-five year career. I went into medicine with the hope of helping those in need, and I am eternally grateful for the opportunity to do just that, at least in a modest way.

Medicine has changed a great deal since I first started. We now have CT scans, endoscopy (fortunately or unfortunately that does include colonoscopy), MRI scanning, and minimally invasive surgery. But showing love for those we serve will never change. Holding the hand of a distressed patient in the examination room, telling a bad joke to lighten up the often somber mood in the hospital, or saying a prayer with a spiritual family are the intangibles in medicine that help heal the human spirit.

About ten years ago, I had an experience that I couldn't explain logically. I woke up in the morning knowing that one of my patients, Taylor Johnson, needed a lung scan. I don't know why I thought that. It really did not make any sense. Taylor was suffering with undiagnosed abdominal pain, not chest or lung pain.

On a trip to Louisiana, Taylor had developed severe right upper abdominal pain, classic for gallbladder. He paged me from Louisiana, and I advised him to go to an emergency department, where he had some blood tests and a gallbladder ultrasound. All were normal. Then I saw him in the office when he returned home, and I ordered some additional blood tests and a special liver and gallbladder scan to help further diagnose what appeared to be gallbladder disease. All those tests were normal, yet his pain continued.

That I had such a strong feeling about the need for a lung scan simply was not reasonable. This was clearly *not* a lung problem, but I could not get the thought out of my mind. So I took the unusual step of calling Taylor on the phone at seven in the morning, before hospital rounds.

"You need a lung scan today," I told him. After the words left my mouth, I blushed at the boldness of my statement. I am usually not that direct, but I felt a sense of urgency that I really could not explain.

After a stunned silence, Taylor replied, "I'm sorry, but I'm leaving for Denver this afternoon, and I need to pack and be at the airport by two."

I paused for a minute, searching for what to say next. Some time in my medical career, I had learned the value of negotiation, so I asked, "If I can get the scan in before noon, would you go?"

Another silence at the end of the phone line. Then came a reluctant, "Okay."

I felt relieved, but I wasn't sure why. Next I called the radiology department, something my nurse would normally do. "Could I get a CT contrast study of the chest before noon?" I asked.

A suppressed laugh greeted my request. "Our studies are booked out through the end of the week!" was the reply.

Then silence on my part.

This must have been enough for the technician in the radiology department to cave in, because he said, "Okay, send him right over."

I called Taylor back and gave him the news. He could have the test and then be back by midmorning to pack. I still felt a little strange placing so much emphasis on a study I had difficulty believing was indicated! That was until I heard back from the radiologist two hours later.

"Taylor Johnson has a massive pulmonary embolus in his right lung near the diaphragm," he said. "That's probably why he had such bad abdominal pain and not chest pain. Good call to order a lung scan. You probably saved his life!"

I had to sit down because my knees were suddenly weak. Had Taylor flown out that day and had another blood clot, it may have been fatal. I immediately admitted him from the radiology department to the intensive care step-down unit of the hospital. We discovered a hereditary clotting disorder which predisposed him to pulmonary emboli. He is now on lifelong blood thinners and doing well.

I was so moved by this act of what I could only consider divine intervention that I started to ask my physician friends if they had ever had similar experiences. What I discovered was both surprising and inspiring. Many, particularly those with more gray hair, had personal stories to tell about experiences with no scientific explanation. And they were happy to share them with a colleague who would not criticize them.

I became a good listener. Some of the stories were so amazing that when I retold them to my wife or a friend, I literally had to stop to compose myself. Many gave me chills and goose bumps. After hearing five or six of these incredible experiences, I felt compelled to write them down. This was the birth of my book, *Physicians' Untold Stories*, featuring ordinary doctors in private practice who experienced or witnessed events that could not be explained by anything we learned in medical school.

It is my hope that anyone reading this collection of stories will know with as much certainty as I do that there is something more than what we can see with our eyes, and that prayers are important and may be answered immediately and sometimes in spectacular ways. And most of all, I want everyone to realize that there is hope for those who suffer, because I have witnessed an unconditional love that acts in our day-to-day lives. I want patients to know that many doctors have spiritual as well as scientific sides. It is acceptable to speak with medical professionals about intimate spiritual feelings, because healing sometimes takes place *without* medicine, through a faith that is important and real. I have experienced this and so have many other doctors.

I hope you are touched by these true physician stories as much as I have been and that they bring you inspiration, an inner peace, and hope in this troubled world.

Scott J. Kolbaba, MD
Wheaton, Illinois
2016

Part One
Divine Intervention

~

CHAPTER 1

IF I HAD BEEN BUCKLED

~⌒

LUIS MANRIQUE, MD

THE LIGHT WAS IMPERCEPTIBLE AT first, and I am not sure I recognized that it was a light at all, until it grew brighter and brighter and filled the entire room. It was the middle of the night, and I was lying in my bed sleeping. At least I thought I was sleeping. I was afraid that if I opened my eyes, it would cease being a dream and become real, so I kept my eyes closed. In retrospect, it probably wasn't the rational thing to do, but it seemed logical at the time.

The head of my bed was against the back wall, so when I heard a man's voice from behind me, I couldn't understand where it was coming from. It made me anxious at first, but the voice was so gentle that it reminded me of a loving father comforting a frightened child, and his speech was accompanied by a wisp of air, like a soft touch on my forehead.

"Everything is going to be all right," he said.

The room was so quiet that I slowed my breathing to prevent the sound from interrupting the rest of the message, but there were no other words. And just as quickly as the light appeared, it faded into the blackness of the night, and I drifted off into a deep sleep.

When I awoke in the morning, I was surprised that the dream remained in my consciousness as distinctly as when it happened. Most of my dreams fade away when I open my eyes and start the day. I paused to search my mind for some deep spiritual meaning, but the significance was not forthcoming, and my mental rambling was soon replaced by the reality of preparing a quick breakfast before hurrying off to class.

I was a sixth-year medical student living in Lima, Peru. In my homeland, medical school is actually eight years, combining undergraduate college with medical school. The sixth year is primarily lectures during the day and homework all evening. I had become an expert student, but there was more to learn than I ever thought possible. This had been a very tiring week with many late nights. Now it was Friday, and I looked forward to taking one night off to spend some leisure time with my classmates.

After the final lecture of the day, I headed home to change, and then four of us met at a local nightclub. We must have been a sorry sight, each with dark circles from lack of sleep, but we all were determined to keep up with the usual nightclub crowd. Just after midnight, we could not stay awake and agreed to leave. My friend, Manuel, was our designated driver, although I'm not sure why since he had as many beers as the rest of us. When we walked out of the smoky room into the cool night air, we all gained a second wind.

On our trip back, we rolled down our car windows, and our boisterous laughter echoed off the nearby buildings. As we approached a bridge over a highway crossing, Manuel got into our festive mood and began to swerve back and forth. At first it was fun, but I became nervous sitting in the passenger's seat in the front, and I reached over to fasten my seat belt. Manuel looked directly at me and said, "You don't need to buckle." It was so uncharacteristic for him to say anything like that and with such authority that I immediately released the belt.

Those were the last words that Manuel ever spoke.

At the end of the bridge was a sharp turn, and by the time I realized we were going too fast, Manuel was already into the turn. The tires screeched as we slid into the curb, and then rolled over and over. The driver's door flew open, and Manual, who was already unconscious, was thrown out of the car. He remained in a coma until his death five days later in the hospital. We all screamed as the car careened to a precarious stop upside down on the highway. I had been thrown into the driver's seat behind the mangled steering wheel. When I looked over to where I had been sitting, I felt a sudden chill. The roof of the car had collapsed, crushing the passenger's seat. If I had been buckled, I would have been killed.

I crawled out the window and ran to a nearby fire station for help. Between gasps, I related our tragic story to the fire fighters, who rushed me into the ambulance to direct them to the scene of the accident.

When we arrived, all I could do was to sit down on the curb with my arms outstretched to prop up my body, which was quivering from adrenalin. The severity of the accident finally registered in my brain. One of the paramedics came over to treat me for any wounds I had sustained. I was covered with broken glass from the shattered windshield, but I had no lacerations or broken bones or anything serious. In fact, I was completely unharmed!

Suddenly the prior evening's words came rushing back into my consciousness: "Everything is going to be all right."

Now I knew. A spiritual being had uttered that prophetic statement and inspired Manuel to save my life with his powerful last words.

I went home, still trembling in the quiet of my bedroom, and offered this humble prayer, "Dear Father, thank you for giving me a second chance and for protecting me from harm. Amen."

CHAPTER 2

GOD'S EMISSARIES

~

HAROLD P. ADOLPH, MD

OUT MY WINDOW I WATCHED as a hesitant orange globe rose above the eastern horizon, shimmered off the lake, and cast a long shadow from our mountain to the north. The birds were coming alive and starting to feed on the corn and sorghum crops in the farm fields that checkered the landscape. Along the lot lines separating the fields grew wild eucalyptus trees, giving off a pungent perfume. Here I was, part of the ecology of Africa, living my dream to help relieve the suffering of the poorest of the poor in southern Ethiopia. But I was exhausted.

Before starting in the morning, I always prayed for God's help in carrying out His work. But today, for the first time, I had to deviate from my traditional humble supplication.

"Heavenly Father," I prayed, "I have been a faithful servant for these past seven months, and I hope I have done Thy will, but, Father, I cannot go on. I need an experienced, well-qualified surgeon to take over my position and give me a break. If You cannot send someone to help me today, I cannot go on. Please, please send help. Amen."

Across the street stood my hospital, built from mud and straw blocks whitewashed to give a sanitary appearance. The hospital held 115 beds, but I was the only doctor for thousands of people from all over the country who came to see me with the end stages of some of the most deforming diseases imaginable. Many were at the brink of death and would not survive without emergency treatment or surgery. I had two operating rooms but only one equipped with electricity and a light bulb, with the other relying on the sunlight from outside to illuminate the surgical field. Both rooms had been bustling six days a week with emergencies on Sunday for the last seven months without a break. Not surprisingly, I suffered mental and physical exhaustion. I was ready to give up.

I always felt that my calling was to become a missionary doctor; it was my way of giving back for the abundant blessings I had been given. I was now thirty-two and had completed medical school at the University of Pennsylvania, served my residency in an American hospital in the Panama Canal Zone, and then completed a two-year surgical preceptorship at the Cannon Junior Memorial Hospital in North Carolina. My training was not the typical general surgical track but included rotations in orthopedics, obstetrics, thoracic surgery, and neurosurgery to help prepare for every imaginable problem in a third world country where I would be the only surgeon in the hospital. Our two children, ages six and eight, enjoyed their adventures traveling the world and were home schooled by my patient wife. My contract with the faith-based sponsor of our hospital and four other hospitals in Ethiopia required that I raise a large portion of the funds from personal savings, from friends, and from philanthropic organizations. Before

I left for Ethiopia, I had completed my rounds with family members and others who had generously donated enough to cover my first five years.

When I arrived, I joined a well-loved surgeon who had been in Ethiopia for twenty years. I admired his dedication and perseverance. Surprisingly, we resembled each other so strongly that longtime patients thought I was his son. This went a long way toward establishing my credibility with patients. He agreed to mentor me for five years while I learned the language and the culture, but after eight weeks he was reassigned to another private, church-sponsored hospital, and I was on my own. I was the medical and surgical team, hospital administrator, and educator! I even administered and monitored the anesthesia during surgery. I don't know how I held it together at the beginning, but I had the support of a great nurse and several Ethiopian trainees who were learning to be nurse practitioners.

A typical day started at dawn with seven or eight surgeries, and then I spent the remainder of the time in the clinic. Sometimes we saw as many as a hundred patients in a day. Emergencies punctuated the schedule so frequently that they almost became the norm. At night, a regular stream of travelers arrived, having started their walking sojourn in the early morning. The entourage typically consisted of the ailing family member on a stretcher and ten to fifteen family members who took turns carrying the stretcher along dirt roads and over rivers and streams, often without bridges.

A common surgical emergency at night was a pregnant woman, unable to deliver, who ruptured her uterus. They were often unconscious in shock from loss of blood, and since our blood bank consisted of willing donors (our "walking blood bank"), they required three or four liters of IV fluid before I could even consider operating. This made for a long day that was then repeated over and over again, seven days a week.

After seven months of this I was at my breaking point, and it was then that I offered my desperate prayer for an assistant. I was frankly surprised at the boldness of my request, and I felt guilty, but I knew this would be my last day if I did not get relief. With a tear in my eye and a bowed head, I walked across the street to make rounds, and then scrub for my first surgical case, a patient with a massive goiter (enlarged thyroid) in his neck that extended down behind his breastbone and into his right upper lung. I was familiar with chest surgery, but it was not my specialty, and I wished I had a thoracic (chest) surgeon to help.

As I started the case, my wishful train of thought was interrupted by an urgent knock on the operating room door. An assistant opened the creaking white door to reveal my wife. She never came to visit me here because she fainted at the sight of blood, but, today she stood there boldly.

Behind her stood a man with strikingly black hair as unkempt as his wrinkled clothing, but he greeted me with a broad smile that was contagious. When our eyes met, my knees became weak. A sense of spiritual destiny filled the operating room. I knew immediately that this person was God's emissary, sent to answer my desperate prayer offered just hours before.

"Harold," my wife said excitedly, "I want you to meet Dr. Ivan Moskowitz from Brooklyn, New York. Harold, he has come to relieve you!"

Overcome with emotion, I stood there for several seconds before I could even speak. I wanted to say something profound to express my realization that I had just been touched by a divine hand, but all I could muster was an anticlimactic, "I am very pleased to meet you. If you wouldn't mind waiting, I will finish my case and show you around." Things were a blur after our meeting, but I did remember our conversation when I asked about his specialty.

"Thoracic and cardiovascular surgery," he replied. "In fact, I saw you completing a thyroid case, and I just published a paper on the care of goiters which extend behind the breastbone and into the chest."

It was the very case I had operated on this morning! Now I was beginning to understand the true depth of the miracle unfolding before me.

"How did you happen to come to relieve me?" I asked.

"It was just a series of coincidences," he said. "I always wanted to go on a mission to use my training to help others in need, and when I was nearing the two-year mark of my surgical practice in New York, I awoke one day and knew that this was the time. Not knowing where to go in the third world," he said with a smile, "I used the scientific method! I spread a map of the world on a table, closed my eyes, turned the map around three times, and put a finger down. You guessed it! Ethiopia! I picked up the phone and arranged for a one-month sabbatical to any hospital in Ethiopia. My flight, several weeks later, was to the capital city of Addis Ababa. From there, I did what every thoracic surgeon with a well-organized itinerary would do; I looked in the phone book. My eyes were drawn to a small entry listing your mission headquarters, and I dialed the number. Your mission director, who answered the phone, was delighted to have help for one of his five hospitals, and he randomly assigned me to work with you. I took the next refurbished DC–10 to your grassy airstrip, and here I am!"

I learned later that our mission director was unaware of my desperate situation, since our communication was marginal at best, so his decision to send Dr. Moskowitz to me was truly "random." Yet this "coincidental doctor" went on to heal not only my thyroid patient whom I had worried about that morning, but hundreds of other native Ethiopians.

Dr. Moskowitz provided coverage for me while I went on a one-month rest at one of Africa's lake resorts where I recovered my strength and was able to continue my dream for what turned out to be another forty-two years. After my initial experience, however, I determined to take an automatic one-month break for every five months of work.

Several years later on one of my trips to raise money in the United States, I visited Dr. Moskowitz at his New York hospital. The subway system in New York was confusing to a transplanted African used to navigating jungle roads using the sun and stars. My wife and I with our two children were totally lost when an unusually tall young man approached us—so tall he looked like he could have played for a professional basketball team.

"Do you know where you're going?" he said in a kind, caring voice.

We shook our heads and shared our destination with him.

"If you follow me," he said, "I will take you there."

I'm not sure why he took such an interest in our dilemma, but he became our guide through an underground labyrinth, transferring us from train to train until we came to our destination station, where we all exited. Standing at the long stairway going up to the street level, our guide instructed us to go two blocks straight ahead and then two blocks to the left. Relieved, I started running up the stairs, until I realized I had not thanked our stranger. I turned around to wave and say thanks, but he was gone! There was no exit from the stairway except to the street in front of us or onto a train, and no trains had come in that brief interval. I bowed my head in thanks for God's servant who showed us the way.

My experiences with Dr. Moskowitz represent a very special time in my life. I now know that when I struggled the most, I was the closest to my Creator. When I felt I could not take another step on the grueling Ethiopian path or find my way on a busy New York subway, He was there, and He carried me. Now that I am older and no longer able to continue a mission in Africa, I know that He continues to guide my path, and, when I finally complete my journey, He will be there to carry me home.

CHAPTER 3

MUSIC IN THE EMERGENCY DEPARTMENT

~‿

ROBIN MRAZ, MD

"THERE'S BLOOD EVERYWHERE FROM AN arm wound that's still hemorrhaging," radioed the paramedics who were at Cleveland Manning's home. "He's unresponsive and in shock, and we are ten minutes away."

Cleveland Manning was a kind and hardworking man who lived with his wife in a modest home in the Chicago suburbs. His children were grown and out of the house, and he was now a well-loved grandfather. The minor surgery performed two days before on his left arm was to make a connection between two blood vessels. It is usually a routine procedure, but, in Cleveland's case, a suture came loose, and his artery started spurting blood so rapidly that he was unconscious from the loss of blood within minutes. When his wife found him unresponsive on the living room floor, she ran to call 911.

The paramedics arrived on the scene within minutes and radioed his condition to our emergency department (ED). I was the doctor on duty that day, and when I overheard the message, I hoped they could get him to us before he died. I also hoped I could stabilize the patients who were already here before everything was put on hold to take care of our newest arrival. Things in the ED are not always fair. The first to arrive may be the last seen, depending upon the urgency of the problem. And Cleveland's arrival would certainly trump every other patient waiting for our attention that night.

He would need multiple units of blood, which we normally crossmatch for each individual, but, in absolute emergencies, we use the "universal donor," which is O negative. This was one of those occasions. I called to our charge nurse, Cindy Conte, to send someone to the blood bank to pick up two units of O negative and make sure there were at least two more available. Then I hurried back to my last two patients to do as much as I could in the eight minutes now remaining.

I didn't accomplish much before Cleveland made his spectacular entrance through the double doors of the ambulance bay. I will never forget the scene. He was lying flat on his back on a gurney with a paramedic straddling his body, actively doing CPR while calling out the cadence for the chest compressions. Another paramedic was holding Cleveland's wrist, attempting to keep the bleeding to a minimum, although not as successfully as I would have expected, since Cleveland was lying in a pool of blood. His face looked like a ghost! He had no pulse, no blood pressure, and was completely unresponsive. He was essentially dead.

I remembered a similar situation in training when we were able to bring a patient back with multiple transfusions, but Cleveland had been gone for at least twenty minutes. Looking at him, I was not optimistic, but there was a nagging voice in my head telling me to try.

"Let's go for it," I said to my ED team.

One nurse took over the CPR compressions; another applied pressure to his arm wound, and the IV team started a second IV. I opened the transport box and took out the two units of O negative blood. It comes in plastic bags, which we connected to Cleveland's IV tubing and squeezed as hard as we could to force the blood into his body as fast as possible. Dr. Franklin, our vascular surgeon on call, was also waiting in the ED. He quickly inspected the wound and decided surgery would be the only way to repair the torn blood vessels, but he doubted Cleveland would survive to go to the OR. After applying another pressure dressing, which temporarily stopped the bleeding, he left for rounds.

Cleveland was still unresponsive and without a pulse or blood pressure. After the first two units were squeezed in, we hung another two. I then reached for his carotid artery to see if I could feel anything.

A pulse! I felt a pulse, although it was very weak. It took another two hours before we felt like we were out of the woods. He received more units of blood than I can recall, liters of saline solution, and multiple medications to control his heart rhythm and blood pressure.

Finally, there was a flicker of his eyelids, and Cleveland opened his eyes. He was dazed and could not talk at first, but, over time, I could see his strength coming back. I was thrilled when he finally spoke.

"You guys really have beautiful music here," were his first words. "I want to hear it again. Could you get me back to that room where they play the music? It was so peaceful."

I smiled. "Mr. Manning," I said, "we don't play music in the ED!"

Cleveland went on to describe a beautiful white room with quiet music from instruments that were unfamiliar to him. He sat up to look for the room and was upset when we could not move him back.

My nurse, Cindy, and I had goose bumps when we both realized what had just happened.

Cleveland soon stabilized enough to go to surgery, where the tear in his artery was successfully repaired. He left the hospital several days later, but I saw him again in nine months when he returned to the ED for an unrelated illness. His color was much better this time. I chatted with his wife, who told me she thought he died the last time he was here but came back to life. Cleveland was still arguing with her about where she brought him after he lost consciousness in his home.

"Of course I brought you to the hospital," she said defiantly. "Where else do you think I would bring you?"

But he was still not totally convinced. I had to agree with Cleveland. He *was* somewhere else for those three hours, a place that was so beautiful and peaceful he longed to return, a place of purity and comforting music, a place where we all hope to go someday—a place called heaven.

CHAPTER 4

THE BURNING BUS

~

SCOTT J. KOLBABA, MD

WE SLOWED DOWN ON THE expressway for a closer look at the dozens of flashing lights from police cars and fire trucks. The object of their attention was an incinerated coach bus parked off a blocked exit ramp. "That's Luci's bus!" my wife shouted, gazing at the bus that was still belching great clouds of black smoke. The blood drained from my face as I realized she was right. Our daughter, Luci, had been riding on that bus!

That memorable day started like most did when our high school show choir had an out-of-state competition. A flurry of activity in the morning, taking hair out of curlers, making sure the costumes were packed with all the fittings, and gathering up the makeup, the snacks, and most importantly the earbuds for music. At 2:45 p.m. as planned, I dropped Luci at her high school to join thirty-nine other chatty girls. There they boarded the ill-fated luxury bus headed for Onalaska, Wisconsin, on the shore of the Mississippi River. My wife, Joan, and I followed an hour later with our GPS programmed for the five hour trip.

The bus ride was uneventful until they were about an hour from Onalaska. Then Luci and some of the girls heard a popping sound near the right rear tire. It was not very loud, and, since nothing seemed to happen immediately, they went back to talking, sleeping, and listening to music. At about 8:00 p.m. the noise became louder, so the bus driver decided to pull onto an exit ramp to investigate. He found a flat rear tire, but the heat generated from it caused him concern, and he went back into the bus for the fire extinguisher. In the meantime, the girls waited impatiently inside the bus for the problem to be resolved. A companion bus that was following also pulled off, and the members of the troop were watching the activity when they noticed something so alarming that they grabbed their phones and sent a series of urgent texts to everyone in the disabled bus.

"Your bus is on fire! Get out!"

The flat tire had generated enough friction to cause a fire, and now the flames were visibly licking at the side of the bus. Seeing the flames and smelling the smoke, the girls started to scream, "Get off; get off!" Everyone sprang to their feet and pressed forward toward the congested single front door. The fire progressed quickly, and soon the entire bus filled with such dense clouds of smoke that the girls could not even see their feet. Those who were shoeless felt the heat on the floor as the flames darted along the underside of the bus. Luci and her friends, who were seated in the back, sobbed as they waited at the end of the slow-moving line. Would they ever see their families again?

The flames were now wrapped around the bus like a deadly blanket while the girls were still far from escaping what could soon become a giant burning coffin.

Then something amazing happened. It was as if a large hand moved silently over the bus, dampening the flames enough to allow each of the forty girls to escape totally unharmed. Thirty-seven, thirty-eight, thirty-nine, forty! The stunned students in the second bus watched as the last girl leaped to safety just as a roaring wall of flames engulfed the interior, consuming everything—except the girls!

Luci, now on the crowded number two bus, called us on her cell phone. "I'm safe; I'm safe," she said over and over, and then silence, punctuated by what sounded like sobs. "There was a little fire on the bus," she said, obviously minimizing the true situation to spare us anguish, "but I am safe and everyone is fine. I can't talk anymore and have to go," she said, and she hung up.

Shaken by the news but relieved no one had been hurt, we continued driving. When we finally passed the scene an hour later, we were shocked to see the reality of the disaster and the smoking shell of the gutted bus. We tried to stop, but the police wouldn't allow us to take the blocked exit, so we drove on to meet our daughter at the hotel in Onalaska. Finally, just after one in the morning, the girls arrived. Luci was too traumatized to talk about what happened and went straight to bed. Relieved to have our little girl alive and unharmed, we let her go.

Still, we feared for the competition. All of the custom-fitted costumes, shoes, makeup, and undergarments had been completely destroyed. Would the girls still compete, and, if so, would they have to sing in their rumpled, slept-in, day's-old clothes?

At close to two that morning, we were unwinding in the hotel lobby with many of the parents when we heard the announcement. "We are going to compete in the morning!

We're not letting this stop us," said Kelsey Nichols, our young choir director.

My wife, Joan, who was in charge of the costume committee, was just as surprised as I was. We had no costumes, shoes, makeup, or undergarments, and, even if we did, how could we have them fitted in the nine hours between two and the performance at eleven?

But Director Nichols's statement provoked a flurry of activity. While the girls slept, parents and alumni of the show choir who had heard about the disaster brought clothing to the home of Mike Moukheiber, a parent and the president of the organization. Then Diane, his wife, with a contingent of parents and students made a 3:00 a.m. raid on the high school. Fortunately they were accompanied by the principal, Dave Claypool, who coincidently had a girl in the choir and who also had the keys. They rummaged in dusty storage closets until they found twenty-five old sequined costumes, which they loaded onto cars for the trip to Wisconsin. But that was not enough for the troop of forty.

Miraculously, when Joan and I arrived at the changing room at eight that morning, a student from the host school, Onalaska High, wheeled in another twenty-five sequined costumes they had also found in their storage cabinets. Now we had fifty costumes for the forty girls, but could they all be fitted in three hours?

In the meantime other parents made regular runs to the local Walmart for makeup, undergarments, duct tape, Scotch tape, and feel-good snacks. The homeroom was alive with mothers and girls trying on ill-fitting costumes. My wife was supervising the fittings with generous amounts of silver duct tape and safety pins. She was cutting and sewing and taking in and out seams. When I saw her come up for air, she was drenched in sweat.

Girls from all twelve schools at the competition and their directors and parents stopped by regularly to see how they could help. "This is what heaven must look like!" one of the mothers declared as she witnessed the kindness exhibited that morning.

We still had to deal with the lack of shoes, and we could not perform on the risers without them. But before we had time to panic, our host school located a closet with dozens of tan high-heeled shoes for our girls. In addition, performers from competing schools and coaches who heard about the "burning-bus school" showed up and literally took off their own shoes for us to use. It was such an act of generosity and kindness that it brought my wife to tears.

During their brief warmup in the fitting room at ten thirty, several girls lost their tops, so my wife had to attach all the straps with more duct tape and pray they would hold during the actual performance.

At eleven, twelve hours after the devastating fire, the girls filed onto the stage, half in sequined purple costumes and half in beautifully contrasting silver, and all with shoes. The master of ceremonies announced that just hours before, this group of girls was in a burning bus and that their costumes were all destroyed, but with determination and a heroic effort, they overcame all obstacles and were ready to perform. A spontaneous cheer came up from the audience.

Then a hush fell over the stadium as the girls began to sing Jimmy Eat World's stirring anthem from "The Middle":

"Little girl, you're in the middle of the ride, everything, everything will be just fine, everything, everything will be all right."

Their song about overcoming adversity and persevering had been selected months before, and now they knew why. It fit perfectly with the series of coincidences that punctuated that fateful trip. The girls performed with such beauty and passion that there were few dry eyes in the audience.

At the end of the day came the award ceremony. There were outstanding schools from all over the Midwest. Second place went to one of those schools and then first place. Even if our girls did not win, they were reassured that they had done their best under unbelievable circumstances. But that wasn't the end.

"Now for the grand champions," announced the master of ceremonies as the stagehands lifted a trophy nearly as tall as many of the girls.

"The winner—Wheaton-Warrenville South Esprit, having overcome a bus fire to do the impossible! Congratulations!"

A standing ovation followed, with both cheers and tears for the group of girls, their parents, and the director who refused to give up, and for the series of miraculous events that brought us to that unforgettable moment.

Back in the homeroom, no words were needed. I just hugged Luci.

PART TWO
DEATH AND THE AFTERLIFE

~

CHAPTER 5

GRANDMA O'HANLON

~

JOHN A. HEITZLER, MD

MY WIFE, JOAN, WAS BIRTHING our fifth child with her attending obstetrician, two nurses, and me in the delivery room, when a quiet, unassuming midwife, Johannah O'Hanlon, stepped in and, without saying a word, saved Joan's life.

In order to understand the significance of this miracle, you need to know a little more about the background of this exceptional midwife. Johannah O'Hanlon was Joan's grandmother. As a young lady, she and her two brothers were sent to the safety of the United States from Ireland by their father, Michael. Michael regularly skirmished with English soldiers, rode on horseback at midnight on illegal missions, and hid Catholic priests in secret rooms in his home. It was a time of great danger, and Michael feared for the lives of his family, particularly his special daughter, Johannah, who demonstrated remarkable charity to all the rebels who crossed their threshold in the dark of the night.

After immigrating to the United States, she lived with her uncles on a farm in Sterling, Illinois, until her new home could be constructed by her two brothers and her betrothed.

When the home was completed, she married and moved into the bustling Irish community in Chicago. She gave birth to her first child, a son, who lived only six months and died of complications of pneumonia. She took in laundry for a time until after the birth of her second child, a daughter, Marie. When Marie was two, Grandma O'Hanlon became a midwife and stayed with her families for up to six weeks after a birth. She took Marie with her and tutored her when they were away from home. Marie became a beautiful young lady and found the love of her life, married, and moved into their own home in the Chicago suburbs.

Grandma O'Hanlon continued her service to others as a midwife, but, when her husband died in his sixties, the family encouraged her to move in with Marie, who now had a child of her own, Joan (my future wife). There, the love that Grandma O'Hanlon and Joan shared ultimately bonded them in a way that would overcome the boundaries of time and space. Joan often said that when she got into trouble with her mother, if she could make it to Grandma O'Hanlon's lap, she'd be safe.

Grandma O'Hanlon continued to serve as a midwife, but, at the time, there was considerable prejudice against the Irish population in Chicago, so she was primarily involved with delivering babies in the Irish community on Chicago's south side. If her service was needed and the family could not pay, she gladly worked for free. I remember one grateful family with very little money, but Grandma O'Hanlon was named in their will. The lot in Chicago near the Dan Ryan Expressway that she inherited after the couple died turned out to be very valuable.

Grandma rode the train into the city and got off near Madison Avenue. In those days, there were many homeless men on the streets, and she always had something for them. Her friends thought she was foolish to give money to the homeless because they would often use it to buy alcohol, but Grandma simply said that she did what God would want her to do, and what the men did with the money was up to them. She became a spiritual model for the entire family.

Joan's fifth pregnancy proceeded uneventfully, and, when the ultrasound revealed that we were expecting another boy, we decided to name him Michael, after Grandma O'Hanlon's father. She would like that.

Labor contractions started on March 14, and, on the fifteenth, the Ides of March, we went to the hospital. I called my partner, Dr. Michael Hussey, to do the delivery. With contractions coming closer and closer, Joan was moved to the delivery room where there was a flurry of activity to make sure their busiest obstetrician (me) would not be disappointed with his own team. I tried to maintain my role as husband and father and not participate as an obstetrician. Everything went well, and Joan delivered a healthy baby without anesthesia or pain medication. After the delivery, the routine in those days was to manually explore the uterus to make sure no part of the placenta was remaining. During that procedure, Joan began to experience considerable pain.

To lessen her pain during the procedure, Dr. Hussey suggested she be given the standard drug at the time, Trilene, which is administered by mask to induce a deep sleep. Joan hesitated to accept it because she did not want to become unconscious, but she finally agreed. As the nurse was about to put the mask over her face, Joan looked up and saw Grandma O'Hanlon, who had just come into the room and stood at the foot of her bed. She was dressed in her typical blue dress with tiny white polka dots and a gray knit sweater vest. Her hair was white and put up in a bun on the top of her head. She didn't say a word but stood there, shaking her head, with her arm on her hip and a look of displeasure on her face. Joan realized immediately that her beloved grandmother did not want her to accept the anesthetic, so she pushed the mask away.

No one remembered that Joan had eaten a large meal before she went into labor, and two minutes after refusing the anesthesia, which would have put her into a deep sleep, she suddenly vomited the large meal. Had the mask been on her face, she could easily have choked and aspirated into her lungs, which could have killed her.

Grandma O'Hanlon, without saying a word, slipped out of the delivery room as quickly as she arrived, her mission complete, her presence unnoticed by anyone else in the room. Joan made it to the safety of her lap one more time, their unconditional love transcending all earthly bounds—because Grandma O'Hanlon had died twenty-two years before.

CHAPTER 6

MARY'S *CHRISTMAS CAROL*

∼

DAVID MOCHEL, MD

SHE WAS DEAD; NO QUESTION. Eyes closed, no pulse, no heart-beat, no respirations, no movement, and unresponsive. I don't know how it happened. It was a routine ankle surgery. Mary was given general anesthesia and went to sleep, but when her antibiotic was given intravenously, she arrested. Her monitor showed a flat line, and I immediately called a "Code Blue."

The operating room was suddenly filled with people. Our scrub nurse initially started to do CPR, but Mary was over three hundred pounds, and my nurse was not tall enough to adequately do compressions. One of the OR techs with strik-ingly red hair rushed in from the room next door and took over. Young and relatively inexperienced, the red-headed tech was not doing the compressions well enough to generate a pulse, so I asked him to step aside. He did not move. I asked him again, but again, no movement.

I still couldn't feel a pulse. In the heat of the moment, politeness is sometimes compromised. I gently but firmly elbowed him out of the way. The tech stumbled away, and I took over. I had to do the compressions forcefully in order to achieve a pulse, and, in so doing, I felt her sternum and possibly one rib crack. After several minutes and some cardiac meds given intravenously, Mary regained a heartbeat and started to breathe on her own. She did not wake up until after she was transferred to the intensive care unit. Cardiologists took over and multiple tests were done, including a coronary angiogram, but nothing revealed the cause of her arrest. We assumed it was a reaction to the antibiotic.

Mary was a little dazed for several days, but she eventually recovered, and, after one week, she was ready to be discharged. I stopped in on her last day to give some final instructions about the care of her ankle.

Mary had always been a very negative person, and I expected to be blamed for causing her arrest, but her mood surprised me. She was sweet, pleasant, and very respectful.

"Thank you for saving my life," she said in almost a whisper.

Now I had to sit down. This was not the person I operated on. I thanked her for her kindness but told her it really was a team effort.

"No," she said. "I know it was *you!* I watched you from above the operating room. When my heart stopped, I could feel myself floating above my body, and I watched everything. I saw the young orderly with the bright red hair come in from the room next door and do CPR, and then I saw you elbow him out of the way since he would not move when you asked him. You saw him stumble away, didn't you?"

Her statement gave me goose bumps. There was no way she would have known this unless she was right there observing everything in the room.

"Then I saw you have my attending internist paged, and you kept looking at the door over and over waiting for him to appear, but he did not. My grandmother, who passed away years before, came to me and told me that if I was kind and loving, there would be a special place in heaven for me, but this was not my time. I came back when you started to do my CPR."

I didn't know what to say. Her observations of the minutest details of her arrest were things that no one would have known. My mind raced to find a logical scientific explanation for what she was telling me, but I could not. She had not been conscious, her eyes were closed, and she had no logical way of knowing what took place in the OR that day.

I saw Mary back in the office several times after that hospitalization, and each time, she was the most loving and considerate person I could imagine. She was like Ebenezer Scrooge in *The Christmas Carol*. Her near-death experience and her conversation with her deceased grandmother gave her a new outlook on life. She became a joy to her widowed father and to everyone she met. Mary lived only a few more years because of her multiple medical problems, but I know that during that time, she made her grandmother proud and is now in the special place she promised.

CHAPTER 7

A CALL FROM MOM

~

PATRICK C. FENNER, MD

"PATRICK, I DON'T THINK I was a very good mother for you. I think I failed you."

I was a second-year resident in internal medicine at Butterworth Hospital in Grand Rapids, Michigan, when my mother called me with that opening pronouncement. Anyone who knew my mother would know how extraordinarily unusual this was. During my residency, I spoke with her at least every one or two weeks, but she never called me. We did not have cell phones at the time, and she knew that she would never reach me in my apartment because I was always so busy, and when I was not in the hospital, I was probably sleeping.

The most unusual thing about that call, however, was her demeanor. My mother never complained about anything. After I grew up and left home, I realized how hard her life had been, but she was never anything but positive and optimistic. Her statement was so shocking to me that I knew that our roles had now reversed, and it was now my turn to comfort her. I'm not sure I was ready for that responsibility!

Mom had just come through a major gallbladder surgery, which entailed a very large incision through her abdominal muscles, making the recovery long and painful. She was in the hospital five days and called me on Saturday afternoon, the day after she was released. I felt guilty when she called because I had intended to send her flowers, but had somehow never gotten around to it. I also could have taken the time off to visit her in Florida, where she was living, but this was a particularly busy rotation, and it would have required a heroic effort. I hoped she would understand.

The night before she called, I had gotten only three hours of sleep, but I had the entire Saturday off. It was a beautiful spring day, but I was so tired that I could only muster enough energy to watch college sports on TV. At the time, I thought it was a coincidence that she would call on the only day in two months that I was home and awake, and the only day that I could speak with her for longer than fifteen minutes.

"What's wrong, Mom?" I asked.

"Patrick," she said, "I have been having a bad day. I have a horrible feeling that I have been a bad mother and haven't given you what you needed as a son."

"Mom, you were the best mom I could have ever had," I said. I played both football and basketball in high school and college, and my mother came to *every* game I was in. Every one. I'll never forget my first pass play in a college game. I was a receiver, and the coach called a long pass to me. After the snap, I ran on pure adrenalin. A beautiful spiral pass was launched into the air, and I stretched out my arms, grabbing the ball with my fingertips. Then I ran for a total of sixty-three yards and a touchdown. Our fans were on their feet cheering wildly, but I didn't hear them at all because I was looking over to where my mother was in the stands. I always knew where she was. We instantly made eye contact, and I'll remember the unspoken communication for the rest of my life. *I'm really proud of you, Son.* That expression of joy and true love made every struggle worthwhile.

"Do you remember that game?" I asked her, referring to that memorable day.

She knew instantly what I was talking about. "I will never forget it," she said. "I was so proud of you that day. I knew how hard you were working to excel in sports and still maintain your academics. The glow on your face after your pass made my humble efforts to support you suddenly so meaningful."

I could tell that she had been crying when she first called, but the thought of that first college pass must have brought a warm remembrance that brightened her mood.

I was the youngest of three children. I had an older brother who lived just five minutes away from Mom in Florida. My older sister was also out of the home and living in New York. But I think I was her greatest concern. She never told me that and would never admit it, but since I was the baby in the family, and had suffered a serious eye injury when I was three, I had the opportunity to spend more quality time with her than my brother and sister did, and she and I treasured our time together. I was able to share my childhood problems with her, and she always seemed to make me feel better. But she never shared her true feelings with me. Things were always just fine. But now I was seeing a different side. She really was human, with human emotions of pain and uncertainty and regret. This was always hidden while I was growing up.

Now she needed me. I was the one listening to her. I never told her how much I loved her and really appreciated all that she had done for me as a child. She was always encouraging when she needed to keep me on the right path. Because of her, I did well in school and was able to get into a good college and. ultimately, into medical school. She taught me determination and perseverance. She taught me about love and family. She taught me that there was something higher than us. She taught me to use my talents well. She was my example and my hero, and I knew this was the right time to tell her. As I did, the emotions built up in my chest, and a tear ran down my cheek.

"You were the greatest mom anyone could ever have," I blurted again.

There was a long silence on the phone. I think that statement made her cry again, to hear it from me. We had never talked liked this before. I could tell as we spoke that she was at peace with herself and with me.

"Patrick," she said, "I am so glad that we were able to speak like this to each other. I never realized how much you appreciated and loved me." I could sense her mouth quivering with emotion. "Thank you so much for listening to me today. I feel so much better. You have made me feel like my life was truly special for you."

"It was, Mom. I love you more than you know."

"I love you too, Patrick. I am tired now, and I think I will lie down. Goodbye, Patrick."

"Goodbye, Mom. I love you."

"I love you too, Son."

I had trouble putting the phone down. It was as if that feeling of love and peace would go away when I hung up, and I was not ready to get back to the real world. I reveled in the pure emotion that we expressed to each other, until I was interrupted by the ringing of the phone two hours later.

"Hello," I said.

"Patrick, it's about Mom. Something happened!" I recognized the voice of my sister, Sherry.

"No, Mom's fine. I just spoke with her." I said.

"She's not, Patrick. Mom died!"

"No, I just got off the phone with her, Sherry, she's fine."

"She's not. Something's happened. She died, Patrick. She's gone! When Mom hung up the phone after talking to you, she walked into the bedroom and collapsed. Dad called the paramedics, and they brought her to the emergency room, but they were not able to save her."

It couldn't be possible. I had just bonded with my mother in a way I never had before, and now she was gone. I just lost my best friend.

Even though twenty years have elapsed since our conversation, I still become emotional telling her story. But I know what a great gift I was given, to be able to speak my heart on her last call. I think she knew her time was limited. She was always there when I was growing up to help with my awkward transition from child to adult. Now it was my turn to give my mom peace with her transition from mortality—to eternity.

CHAPTER 8

GUS'S LAST SALUTE

~

SCOTT J. KOLBABA, MD
JOHN R. BORN, DO

GUS WAS ONE OF MY favorite patients. I know doctors should
not have favorites, but we all do. He was a patient for thirty
years. I always heard him coming because of his characteristic
limp from World War II injuries. I watched him raise three
wonderful children, finish a successful accounting career,
and then retire. I knew his devoted wife, Lucy, who changed
roles with him as provider when Gus entered the silent world
of Alzheimer's disease. But only after he was bedbound did I
learn of his true heroism. I was visiting him at home (yes, a
real doctor house call!) when I asked Lucy to tell me the story
of his misshapen legs. She sat up in her chair and, with unmistakable pride, related this amazing story.

Gus was an enlisted army corporal making his way inch by
inch through France and into Germany. Fighting was intense
as they crossed the border. Artillery shells rained into the forest throughout the day, and the hazy air was filled with the
acrid smell of burning munitions, vegetation, and decayed
flesh. At dusk there was an eerie silence, and Gus lay down to

rest and talk with his friend, Robert Barnes, while the other members of his platoon stood in a circle, smoking. A sudden scream from a lone artillery shell broke the silence, exploding right in the middle of the standing men. Shrapnel pierced their faces and bodies, and all were killed within seconds. The only survivors were Gus and Robert, since they were not in the direct blast.

Gus was hit in both legs from metal fragments that ripped through his uniform and shattered his bones in multiple places. He lay there among the dead in a pool of blood, unable to stand, hoping for a rescue party before he would suffer the fate of the other members of his platoon. As night fell, his mind was taken off the pain of his wounds by Robert's agonizing groans. Gus could not speak, and Robert had been blown too far out of reach for Gus to comfort him with his touch. Early in the morning, before sunrise, Robert fell silent, and Gus knew that he, too, was dead.

Weak from the loss of blood and in extreme pain because of his fractured legs, Gus held on until reinforcements came upon the gruesome scene hours later. He was stabilized by the medics in the field, and then quickly transported back to the surgical tents, where he was examined by one of the doctors. His legs were so mangled that the doctor knew immediately what must be done. "I'm sorry," he said. "We are going to have to remove both of your legs."

Gus was devastated. In those days, losing his legs would sentence him to lifelong disability. Without legs, he believed he would not be able to provide for a family. Tears came to his eyes.

"Please save my legs," he pleaded over and over. "Please find someone who knows how to put damaged legs back together. I promise I will put up with any surgery and therapy to remain whole!"

The surgeons, touched by his heartfelt plea, spoke with their commanding officer. He knew of a skilled orthopedic surgeon at Fitzsimons Hospital near Denver, Colorado, who might be able to do what Gus was requesting. They arranged for his evacuation to England, where he was transfused and stabilized. After two months of treatment, he was flown back to the United States and into the operating room of Dr. Michael Stanton, a young orthopedic surgeon on the cutting edge of bone grafting and repair. In his two years at Fitzsimons, Gus underwent seventeen operations and extensive physical therapy, which ultimately allowed him to walk out of the hospital. He was left with a lifelong limp and some pain, but he walked!

Between surgeries and rehabilitation at Fitzsimons, he wandered into the kitchen one morning looking for a glass of tomato juice. Waiting there was a pretty young registered nurse named Lucy, and the glass of tomato juice led to a marriage that would span over sixty years.

I asked Lucy if Gus was ever bitter about his lot in life, and she told me just the opposite. Nearly every day he expressed a genuine thankfulness for his life and his legs. I believe he truly was one of the "greatest generation."

When Gus was confined to bed because of Alzheimer's disease, Lucy became his nurse and caregiver, honoring her vow, "for better or for worse." She was his champion with the

Veterans Administration and secured the best rotating bed available and other equipment necessary to prevent bed sores and to treat his recurrent aspiration pneumonias. She hired caregivers, pureed his food, and called me to see him at home whenever he had a change in status.

But even with exceptional care, Gus was aging. He turned ninety on February 14, Valentine's Day (Lucy was born on the same day one year later). His World War II injuries had become reinfected, and I knew this would be difficult to treat and probably impossible to cure.

On a routine Friday morning I was making rounds at the hospital and had just seen my last patient when I answered a page from Lucy at seven. To my sorrow, she informed me that Gus had passed away. After I hung up, by coincidence, I saw my partner, Dr. John Born, coming in from the parking lot. We paused in the doctors' lounge and exchanged news on our patients.

"Lucy called this morning. Gus just died," I told Dr. Born.

His face paled as if he had just seen a ghost. For a few seconds he could not speak.

Alarmed, I asked, "What's wrong?"

"That is so strange." He sat down at the computer station to compose himself. "I was driving into the hospital when I had the overwhelming urge to turn off the radio. I never do that, but I was overcome with the feeling that I was being summoned by a more important call, and my thoughts immediately turned to Gus. I kept having flashbacks on what you had told me about his military career and his life, as if he was saying good-bye."

We checked the time of my page. Seven o'clock, the exact time Dr. Born turned off his radio!

We have since reflected repeatedly on the events of that morning, finally concluding that somehow we were the honored recipients of Gus's last goodbye. I don't know why he picked us, although it would not be unlike him to say thank you to his doctors of over thirty years.

So, to Gus, I say in return, "Thanks for your last salute, my old friend."

CHAPTER 9

FREEZING COLD

~

JOHN P. MENDENHALL, MD

I KNEW I WAS FREEZING to death, because I read about the stages in medical school. First your body starts to feel cold. Then you begin to shiver. That's the body's way of generating heat. As you become more hypothermic (temperature below the normal body temperature), the shivering stops, and you become confused and very tired. They say it is not an unpleasant feeling as you slip off to sleep and then into a coma, and then death.

I had been hiking with the scouts in a branch of the Rocky Mountains with peaks as high as thirteen thousand feet. It was a beautiful fall day, and the hiking was exhilarating. As we hiked higher and higher into the thin air, the scouts were excited about camping on the side of a mountain. I didn't realize just how high we were until I gradually became short of breath. When I couldn't keep up with the troop and started wheezing, I knew that I must have mountain sickness with fluid in my lungs (pulmonary edema). I knew I needed to be at a lower altitude and get medical attention, but we were too far into the wilderness for anyone to come to us quickly. We would have to hike down. At least that was the plan, until we were suddenly engulfed in a mountain blizzard. Walking for me was now impossible.

In between gasps, I spoke with the other adult leaders, and we decided that, for safety, the scouts needed to get off the mountain, and I would remain with my sleeping bag to recover. They would then send a rescue team back to get me out.

They left, and I was glad to be able to rest. At least I could catch my breath when I wasn't moving. I found a relatively peaceful location on the trail sheltered by pines, opened my sleeping bag, and crawled in.

It was still morning, but the temperature continued to drop. As I shifted in the bag, I heard the unmistakable crunch of the snow when it gets very, very cold. I zipped up, put the hood over my head, and curled up as much as I could to take advantage of what warmth my body was generating.

After I had been lying there for only a short time, the shivering started. First my chest tensed, and then my arms and legs trembled before the shivering finally turned into true teeth chattering.

My eyes became heavy as the shivering gradually left, and I became surprisingly comfortable. The gravity of my situation would not register in my brain, and, in a matter-of- fact way, I concluded that this would be a pleasant way to die. I closed my eyes for just one second, and then another, and then…

"Wake up; wake up," said a voice.

I opened my eyes and discovered a forest ranger who had also been trapped by the sudden blizzard. He had been higher in the mountain and was descending on horseback.

I was so disoriented that I was upset that my deep sleep had been interrupted.

"Get up," he said, "and cover yourself with this blanket, and let me help you get on the back of my horse."

It was a bumpy ride down the mountain, but we finally made it to the ranger station. From there they took me to the hospital, where I knew most of the staff. As I regained my senses, I was shocked to see my chest X-ray looking as white as the blizzard that stranded me. I wondered how I could get oxygen at all with so much fluid in my lungs. My recovery was gradual, but I was released several days later, thankful that a ranger with a horse just happened to be where I was in the expansive wilderness of a mountain range.

Years passed, and my near-death freezing experience was just a distant memory. It was a typical work day when I left my house for the hospital at my usual time of five thirty in the morning. I first went to the hospital for rounds, and then into surgery before heading to the office located across the street. This morning, however, I did something I had never done before: I stopped at my office first. I don't know why. I had hospital rounds to do but no work at the office.

I opened the front door and sat at my desk contemplating my day and why I was there, when I was interrupted by an urgent knock on the back door. It was between five thirty and six, and our staff did not arrive until eight. I hurried to open the door. Standing in the cold was a man with tears streaming down his cheeks and an expression of ultimate desperation on his face.

"I have just suffered a terrible loss," he said to me. "My son was hiking in the canyon and got separated from his group. They just found him frozen to death."

I took his hand and we sat down. Between sobs, he went on, "I can't imagine how much he suffered before he died. It must have been terrible. I can't stop thinking about it."

Now I knew why I had come to the office, and, without hesitation, I knew exactly what to say. "I want to tell you a story that will help you," I said.

I related the story of my experience with hypothermia and freezing on the mountainside five years before, and explained in an empathetic way that it was not an unpleasant experience at all, that his son must have been very peaceful before he died, and that he would not have suffered.

The man's countenance changed as he listened intently to my story. By the time I finished, he was calm. We hugged, and he left. It was really quite a short visit. I never learned his name, nor he mine. Later that day, I watched the evening news report that a boy had been found the night before, frozen in a nearby canyon.

I wondered why I had chosen to stop at the office before rounds when I never did before, why the grieving father chose an ordinary back door of all the multiple doors in our medical complex, and why I knew just what to say when I was called upon to speak. My only conclusion is that we were brought together by a loving Creator to provide comfort and peace to an anguished father's soul.

I never saw the father again.

CHAPTER 10

THE ULTIMATE MISSIONARY

~

NOEMI SIGALOVE, MD

THE SILENCE OF THE MORNING was interrupted by the rhythmic clap of my shoes echoing off the concrete walls of the doctors' parking garage. It was five-thirty in the morning, and I was hurrying into the hospital to make quick rounds before leaving on a well-deserved, three-day vacation to Tucson, Arizona. I had no way of anticipating what happened as I passed through the doors of the hospital that morning.

My story started one year before when I first saw Adele Ashton for a minor surgical procedure. Her husband, Ron, always accompanied her. They were in their mid-eighties, and their weathered skin told of long days in the African jungle where they served as physician missionaries. They worked in a makeshift clinic in central Africa, where they spent long hours treating anyone who came to them for help, and then on Sunday they addressed the spiritual needs of the people living in the remote jungle villages. This was the life they knew until age deprived them of the stamina to handle the rigors of treating the desperately ill with minimal medicine and equipment.

I sat in my exam room like a child at the feet of master storytellers, listening in awe of their tales of curing the native people of diseases I had only read about in medical school and of employing surgical procedures I had never performed.

They were so loving and caring that I had to remind myself that I was not the patient. They always asked about my family, my career, my interests, and my life. But what they were most concerned about was my spiritual well-being.

"How are you nourishing your spirit?" Dr. Ron would say. "Are you at peace with yourself and with God?"

If anyone else asked those questions, I would probably be offended, but they always inquired out of love and genuine concern. I think my answers left them with the impression that I knew there was something else to this life, but I certainly did not have their faith. They were the ultimate missionary couple who would do anything to impart the peace they felt from the knowledge of God and the glorious life He offered after death.

I treated Dr. Adele for several more months and always enjoyed our exam room meetings. Although I never saw them out of the context of my office or hospital, I admired their work and their sincere concern for me, and we became good friends. They always had a faith-building story to share, and each one was more inspirational than the one before.

On our last visit, Dr. Ron emotionally expressed his great thankfulness for my care of his dear wife. "Believe and have faith," he said. And he promised, "The truth will become apparent to you in time." I accepted his sincerity but was unsure about his promise.

Adele regained her health, and I did not see my missionary friends again. However, since we were both connected with the same hospital, I was able to receive updates on their lives. I learned that Dr. Ron became ill with cancer, for which he was receiving treatment. I hoped he would respond and recover successfully.

It was March 10, the day I planned to leave on my three-day vacation to Tucson, Arizona. I had not intended to work the morning of the trip, but there was an emergency surgery the day before, and I knew I would need to see my patient post-op early the next morning. So at five-thirty I headed into the hospital.

As the hospital doors opened, an unusual blast of air temporarily took my attention away from the immediate scene, and I found myself on a different plane. In my mind's eye, I saw Dr. Ron. He was standing in a casual outfit, and his eyes seemed to look right into my soul. He was smiling in a way that suggested the fulfillment of a major personal commitment.

Excited to see him, I blurted out, "Hello, friend!" Startled back into reality by the sound of my own voice, I looked around to see if anyone had heard me. Fortunately it was so early in the morning that I was the only one at the entrance of the hospital. I felt a little embarrassed but walked on, wondering why Dr. Ron was on my mind, since I had not thought about the couple for a long time.

I finished my rounds and was soon packing and traveling to the airport. The vacation was quiet and a great stress reliever. The three days went by too quickly, and I soon found myself at Tucson International Airport on my way back. I never check my e-mails on vacation to avoid any distressing news. But now that I was on the way home, I opened my mail-box while waiting for the plane to arrive at the gate.

There was a message from the hospital vice president. As I opened the text, I gasped with emotion. It read, "It is with great regret that I announce the death of Dr. Ron Ashton on March 10. Dr. Ashton valiantly fought a battle with cancer. He was a friend to our hospital and on God's mission serving the poor of Africa with his wife for over fifty years. We will all miss him."

That was the day I left on vacation and the morning he appeared in my mind's eye as I entered the hospital doors. Ron had fulfilled his promise to make the truth apparent that there was something after this life, and the expression on his face made me believe it was the crowning missionary moment of his life.

CHAPTER 11

THE DIME

~ා

STEPHEN J. GRAHAM, MD

I WONDERED IF THE UNUSUAL tattoo on John Walters's arm might be related to the sadness in his eyes. He was seeing me in the emergency department for abdominal pain. I was initially hesitant to ask him about the tattoo, but curiosity got the best of me.

"Is that a coin?" I asked, pointing to his forearm.

"Yes," he said.

"That's a little unusual," I said tentatively, not wanting to offend him.

"It's a dime," he said. "I did it for my son, Robby."

He paused and took a breath. I soon realized why I had struck such a deeply emotional chord.

"He was killed," he said as he stopped again to compose himself. "It was terrible, an accident on the expressway over ten years ago. He was my...only son. He loved coins and had an incredible coin collection. We would go through the change together to find the pennies, nickels, and dimes for his collection books. My wife and I would give him the rarer coins for his birthday and Christmas. His favorite collection was dimes, and he had an unusual knack for finding them everywhere. We would go to a Cubs game, and he would find a dime under his seat or on the sidewalk outside his favorite storefront Christmas window. Whenever we did anything special together, he would find a dime. It was really uncanny.

"I know you probably won't believe this, but after he left us, I started finding dimes too. Anytime I do something that would have been special for him, I find a dime—vacations, dinners out, sporting events. They appear on the floor, under a plate, or anywhere. I can almost count on it now, and I think it's his way of communicating. He looks out for me, like my guardian angel. I wanted Robby to know that I knew he was there, so I put this tattoo on my arm. If you look at it, the year is Robby's birth year, and his name is right here, R-O-B-B-Y."

"That's a touching story," I said, trying not to show my skepticism, while at the same time wishing it really was true. But it was true for John, and that was the important thing.

After I finished his exam, John went for a CT scan, which revealed a minor infection.

"I have good news," I told him after the radiologist called with the report. "You won't need to be admitted to the hospital. It's a simple infection. I'm going to give you some antibiotics, and you need to follow up with your regular physician in three days. Oh, thanks for sharing Robby's story with me," I said as I turned to walk out of his room.

"I had a feeling you could help me," he said. "Thanks."

John's story resonated in my mind, but I still couldn't get myself to accept that a loved one could communicate from the other side.

I made my way back to the doctor's dictation area where patients have no access. As I sat down at my computer to complete his notes, something on the floor caught my eye. I reached for it. *A dime!*

A sudden eerie feeling came over me. Then I smiled.

"Thanks, Robby," I said under my breath, "for looking out for your dad...and for helping me believe."

CHAPTER 12

"GET THE PADDLES!"

~

FRED BOLLHOFFER, MD

"THIS IS GLEN ELLYN AMBULANCE number seventeen on our way, transporting a sixty-two-year-old male with chest pain and EKG changes of an acute anterior MI. ETA twelve minutes. Concerned about his rhythm, frequent ventricular ectopy."

"Okay," the nurse dispatcher replied. "We are opening the door for bay number two. We are ready for you." She looked over at me with a wink and a smile. She knew that as the ED doctor on duty, I was the one who needed to be ready. She also knew that I was already an hour behind, with three patients who would have to wait while I attended our new emergency.

I worried about the paramedic's comment about the patient's rhythm. Usually fairly astute, the paramedic knew that his rhythm could degenerate into ventricular tachycardia or fibrillation, both causing a life-threatening arrest. His comment was a warning.

In exactly twelve minutes, the ambulance pulled into bay number two. As I waited for the gurney to be rolled out and into room A2, the cardiac suite, I tried to finish a few charts on the computer. When I realized no one was leaving the ambulance, I became a little nervous and thought I had better run out to the bay and see what was happening.

Before I even got into the ambulance, I heard the, "One, two, three, four" as a paramedic called out the cadence to his CPR compressions. The worst had happened. The patient's rhythm had degenerated into ventricular fibrillation, and his heart had stopped beating. He had died.

"Get the paddles!" I yelled as I stepped on the rear bumper and grabbed the handle to make my way into the back of the ambulance. Chest compressions stopped briefly as one paramedic rubbed conducting jelly on the man's chest, and the other carefully placed one paddle to the right of his breastbone and the other on his left chest. "Stand clear!"

His whole body lurched as two hundred joules of energy pulsed through his heart. There was a smell of burning hair, but the man immediately sat up and looked around. I breathed a sigh of relief, although I knew we were not out of trouble yet.

"Let's get him into the room!" I said to the nurses, who were now waiting at the doorway of the ambulance.

He was quickly wheeled into the emergency department, but just as he went through the doorway to the cardiac room, the nurse watching his telemetry yelled out, "V. fib."

His heart had stopped again. His eyes closed, and the color drained out of his face, leaving him a ghostly white.

I grabbed the paddles in the room. "Stand clear!"

Again, a sudden lurch, and he opened his eyes and looked around. But he looked as though he was far away, not part of what was happening in his room. He looked much too calm.

"Are you okay?" I asked.

He started to answer, but before he could, his eyes rolled back, and he went limp. His heart stopped for a third time.

I grabbed the paddles one more time. "Clear," I said. I looked around to make sure that no one was touching him or his bed. Again a powerful shock, and his rhythm returned immediately to normal. We hung a bag of IV lidocaine to prevent his rhythm from degenerating again, and he finally stabilized.

His monitor now showed a normal rhythm. The nurses handed me the arrest record to sign. I looked on the paper to see his name, Robert Andrews.

"Hi, Bob," I said. "I'm Dr. Bollhoffer." I shook his hand. It seemed a little anticlimactic to be making introductions to a person we had brought back from the dead three times.

He smiled as politely as he could under the circumstance, and then seemed to drift off again into his own world. I wondered if he was aware of what had happened or if he was so frightened that he was retreating back into his shell. I have been involved with code situations frequently over my years in the emergency department, but never quite like this.

"Bob," I said. "Are you okay?" He didn't answer so I said again, "Are you okay? You should be fine now, but you must have been frightened through that whole experience." I tried to reassure him as much as I could.

"You know, Doc," he said. "I'm not frightened at all, I think because of what I just experienced. When my heart stopped, my older brother came to me right here in this room. I could see him as clearly as I see you. His expression was so calming, but he didn't speak. My father also came in and walked toward me. Then my ex-wife joined him, and she had a similar welcoming expression on her face. They all stood together by my side." Tears welled up in his eyes.

"It sounds like that should have been comforting," I said. "Is that why you were so calm? Will they be visiting you here?"

"That's what's so strange," he said. "When I died and my heart stopped, I think they came to take me home. You see, my older brother, my father, and my wife all died years ago."

PART THREE
HEALING

CHAPTER 13

GONE FISHIN'

~o

JOHN MESSITT, MD

IT WAS HARD TO SEE Bob lying lifeless in bed in the ICU, having suffered a massive stroke and in a deep coma. Bob was my friend. He and I often shared fishing stories in the doctor's lounge in the early morning before rounds. He was in family practice and sometimes used my specialty of obstetrics for difficult deliveries, but I think his real passion in life was fishing. He could tell me what lure to use for every body of water in the country and in some foreign countries too.

"We're planning to remove his life support if there is no progress in three days," said his ICU physician as he walked past the room. "He's totally unresponsive to any stimulus and is essentially brain dead."

Those were chilling words. Bob and I were laughing together several days ago. I sat down alone with my old friend and drew my chair closer to the head of the bed as I touched his hand. I felt helpless. Was there nothing I could do?

As I leaned toward his lifeless body, the words started to come, slowly and quietly at first, like a whisper, and then louder and more boldly.

"Bob," I said, "I want to tell you about my recent fishing trip to the Northwest Territories of Canada.

"We flew into Hay River, Canada, and, from there, took a small one-engine float plane past Great Slave Lake to the Mackenzie River. The location was too remote for landing strips, so we put down on the river." Now I was really getting into the story.

"I thought it would be an enjoyable experience, until we hit the water—and bounced. That was the white-knuckle time as the plane (and I) pitched back and forth. By the third bounce, I decided I was glad I was not a regular commuter." I instinctively looked for a smile on his face, but, of course, there was none.

"When we finally glided to our mooring, I was happy to step onto a solid dock. Our guide unloaded the luggage and accompanied us to our one-room log cabin with a wood-burning potbelly stove in the center for heat.

"The first morning broke with the sun rising over the water and burning the mist off the river. The sky had wisps of clouds, as if a painter had dragged his brush over a deep blue canvas. After a lumberjack breakfast, we walked across the permafrost ground to our boat. We used tiny Daredevil lures, the smallest I had ever seen, for trolling, with only the river current propelling us. Bob, I'm not sure if even *you* have used such tiny lures." My typical fishing "one-upmanship" now brought a smile to *my* face.

"My first cast was with a large eight-inch muskie lure to simply clear the line and make sure there were no tangles. Before I could reel it in, I had my first strike. It was a grayling. The river was full of them, and they were all hungry. They get to be about three pounds and put up quite a fight. Have you ever caught one?" I paused instinctively for a second, almost expecting an answer.

"It seemed like all we had to do is drop the lure in the water, and we had a fish. By the end of the day, my arms were tired from reeling in our catch. We released most of them, but it made for a day like no other. Bob, I'd like you to go there with me someday." I turned to look around the room to make sure no one had entered, but I was still alone with my fishing friend.

I had known Bob for ten years. We never socialized or went fishing together. Our special time was in the hospital setting in the morning, where we became acquainted with not only our fishing stories but with each other's children and grandchildren, their interests, occupations, and aspirations in life. It took a stroke for me to realize just how close we had become. Life's funny like that. You don't appreciate what you have until it's gone. Now my tales were the only way to keep connected, but in ways that I never imagined at the time.

In addition to his family, medicine, and fishing, Bob also loved his greenhouse. In fact, he was so excited about his plants that he once called me at 3:00 a.m. When I answered the phone, Bob had an excited tone in his voice. I got up and was getting ready to get dressed to go in and help him with a delivery, but it was not about any obstetrical emergency.

"John," he said. "This is Bob."

"Yes," I said with a sleepy voice.

"You have to come and see it!" he said.

I thought about what I needed to wear to do a delivery, and then get to the office.

"It's beautiful, and the smell is like nothing you have ever experienced!" he said.

Now I was really wondering what he was talking about.

"My night-blooming cereus is in full glory in the green-house! It only opens at night and just once a year, and this is the night. You have to come and see it."

I put my pants back in the closet and resumed my place in bed with a sigh of relief. "Thanks, Bob," I said. "But I'll see it in the morning. Good-bye."

I just couldn't share his excitement about a flower. But that was Bob. He was passionate about everything.

Every day that I visited him in his ICU bed, I hoped he would miraculously recover, but I knew this wasn't possible. He had been in the unit for three days now with absolutely no progress, and the plan was to take him off life support in the morning. Each day I told him another story. My wife and friends questioned my sanity telling stories to someone who had no chance of hearing, but I had a strange compulsion to continue. It was something I could do, and probably the only thing I could do for my friend.

The last morning of his life I functioned in slow motion. I walked tentatively into the ICU with an empty feeling in my chest. When I entered his room, I realized it was too late. His bed was stripped to the mattress, and the room was dark and empty. He must have died during the night. I felt sad that I couldn't say my last goodbyes to him, but I smiled as I remembered our good times together.

As I shuffled out of the ICU with my head down, I saw one of the nurses at the nursing station.

"What time did Bob die?" I asked.

Her laugh at first seemed inappropriate. "Oh, he didn't die," she said. "He woke up yesterday, and we transferred him to the step-down unit!"

I stood there, unable to process what she just said. It took me a few minutes to realize that, for me, he had just come back from the dead. I hurried to his new room to see him but found that he was down for some tests. Bob was discharged to a rehab facility before I could see him, but just over a week later, I walked into the doctors' lounge, and there he was, just like old times, standing in his usual place, having an oatmeal breakfast.

"Bob!" I said. "You made an amazing recovery!"

"John," he said with a smile as he moved closer to me, "I want to thank...you...for coming to see me...every day." His speech was halting and labored from his stroke, but he obviously had something important to tell me. "You were the only one who...ever talked to me, and you...you don't know how much...how much I looked forward to your...stories. My favorite was...the Northwest Territories...for grayling. You never told me...that one before. It was...your best."

He became emotional as he told me about his experience. He was able to repeat even the smallest details of every story I told him when he was in an apparent coma. I wonder to this day if there was something more in those stories that I didn't comprehend at the time. Is there a time when a person so close to death makes a decision to stay or leave? Could some simple fishing stories, told by a friend, make a difference? I'll never know.

What I do know is that two men, bonded by friendship, met every morning under unusual circumstances to share stories about what they love, and both came away feeling better. I think that's what life is all about.

Bob continued to recover over the next few months and lived for many more years.

If you were wondering, he never made it to the Mackenzie River in Canada to fish for graylings, at least not in this life.

CHAPTER 14

A SERIES OF MIRACLES

~੭

JOHN P. MENDENHALL, MD

IT WAS THE LOWEST POINT in my life. I sat at my desk contemplating the problems I was facing, when my nurse and receptionist came into my office beaming. "Look what someone left on your reception table," my nurse said. What she laid on my desk took my breath away. It was a large gold-leaf frame, and inside was my family tree, also in gold leaf. Each of my ancestors had a glass birthstone. The tree depicted an extensive group of relatives going back to many great-greats. I was at the base of the tree, as if each of my ancestors depended upon me. *How could I give up and let them all down?* I thought.

I was touched beyond words. I could feel a tear well up in my eye, as I turned to my nurse and receptionist to ask if they had seen the stranger who had anonymously brought the package to my office. Both thought they saw Dave Adams's car drive out of my parking lot that morning. I had served on some church committees with Dave, but we were not close friends. How he knew I was at a crossroads in my life, I will never know, but his gift of unselfish love made me realize I could overcome any obstacle, and it turned my life around. I rarely saw Dave again as our lives went separate ways until... well, I'm getting ahead of myself.

As an orthopedic surgeon, I maintained a busy operating schedule, but this particular week was over the top. I happened to be on call much of that week and was looking forward to having the weekend off. In fact, I had been up most of the night in the operating room and was finishing morning rounds on Saturday. It was a great feeling when I called my partner and signed out. I turned off my pager, changed my coat, and headed out of the hospital.

As I passed the doctor's lounge, I thought about getting a soda before I left, but I was distracted and forgot. As I drove away, I decided to stop at a gas station on the way home for a drink. It was about halfway home, just off the expressway. But again, as I was getting ready to pull off, I became preoccupied with whether I had ordered an appropriate medication for one of the patients I had seen on rounds, and I missed the exit. Fortunately the next ramp was to my home. I could wait until I got to my own refrigerator, which was well stocked with cold pop. I would then change into some casual clothes and take a well-deserved nap. As I worked out the plan in my mind, I went right by the exit!

I must be really tired, I thought. I had never done this before. I would have to turn around to get back home. Then I remembered that just off the next exit was another community hospital. I was on staff but almost never operated there because they always seemed to be out of the orthopedic equipment I needed. But they had a great doctors' lounge, and I could make a quick pass for a soda and then go home to bed.

This time, I didn't miss the exit. I was happy to see the tan building just a few blocks away. The doctors' entrance and parking lot were in the back, but, for some reason, I parked on the other side and went in through the front door. I don't remember ever doing that before.

As I entered the lobby and walked down the hallway I heard a desperate plea. "Doc Mendenhall, Doc Mendenhall!" It was the voice of Kathy Staton, the daughter of Dave Adams, who had changed my life with his expression of love and kindness so many years before.

"Doc," she said, still catching her breath from the sprint to my side. "My daughter Judy just had a terrible fall from a zip line, and she broke the forearm bones in both arms. It's terrible. Her arms are all deformed, and she plays the piano and wants to become a concert pianist! They think she may never be able to play at that level again. My father always told me you were the best orthopedic surgeon around, so I knew you would be the only one who could fix her. I'm so thankful you came."

I was totally exhausted, but how could I refuse to do the surgery? The real problem, however, was the hospital. They were almost always out of the right drills, plates, and screws I needed for a sophisticated surgery like this would be. I was trying to decide how to tell Kathy when one of the surgical nurses came down the hall after seeing her injured daughter in the ER. I think she must have read my mind.

"Doc," she said. "I have great news. You know how you always tell us that we don't have the right equipment for your cases? Well, the operating committee decided to encourage more orthopedic surgery by ordering a large set of the finest orthopedic plates, screws, and drill bits. They arrived this morning, and I just picked them up from our surgical supplier. It's everything that you will need."

And it was. Now I knew without a doubt that someone behind the scenes was directing traffic, and all I could do was to hold on for the ride.

I went to the ER with Kathy and examined Judy. She was right. The radius and ulna in both forearms were fractured in multiple places. Her once beautiful arms and hands were twisted and functionless. This would be a major surgery, and I told Kathy it would normally take at least four hours.

I knew the anesthesiologist, Howard Roberts, who was on call for the hospital that day. He came to the ER to see what he was facing, since he didn't want to spend his entire Saturday in surgery. After we scrubbed and entered the operating suite, Howard marked the time on his chart and reminded me that I promised him I could do it in four hours. I nodded.

As he was putting Judy into a deeper sleep, I was able to start on her right arm. I have never had surgery proceed so quickly. Her separated bones almost fell into place. The new orthopedic kit had the state-of-the-art plates and screws that I loved to use. Within forty-five minutes, I had finished her right arm and was starting on the left. That arm went as miraculously as the right. I was done within forty-five minutes again and informed Howard that he could wake Judy up. He nearly fell off his stool. He looked at the clock: 12:35 p.m. He subtracted the start time and recorded a total surgical time of ninety-two minutes. He had never seen anything like this before, and neither had I. When I went out to speak with the family, they were waiting for me at the door. It was great to see my old friend Dave Adams, Kathy's father, who smiled when he saw me.

"I knew you would finish quickly," Kathy said calmly, "and I already know the result." And she was right. Postoperative X-rays revealed that Judy's bones were positioned perfectly.

Her statement capped the most unusual day of my life. It was a day filled with a series of miracles, starting with something that prevented me from getting a drink in my own doctors' lounge and from taking the exits to the gas station or to my home. Then Kathy Staton locating the person she wanted to operate on her daughter just because I chose an entrance I had never used before. Then performing a complex surgery in record time using instruments that were delivered just hours before I needed them. Finally Kathy's entire family standing at the doorway to the surgical waiting room because they knew that I would finish hours before I predicted.

And what about Judy, you ask. Did she ever play the piano again?

Judy made an uneventful recovery from her surgery, but she required extensive physical therapy. Part of the therapy involved making a beautiful quilt for my family. But the real reward for me was receiving the following invitation in the mail nearly two years later:

You are cordially invited to the opening performance of Judith Staton in concert.

She played like an angel!

CHAPTER 15

THE DREAM

~⌐

RICHARD JORGENSEN, MD

"NATIVE AMERICANS BELIEVE THAT IF you dream about someone, you must tell them about your dream. This is how the Earth Spirit communicates with mortal beings."

I thought this was a fascinating revelation from my psychologist friend, Janet Robbins, who believed it. Over coffee at Starbucks, we discussed her philosophy of life, a mix of modern psychology and 1970s free spirit. I tried to think of my last dream but couldn't remember any, but her statement on revealing dreams resonated with me. I thought about it long after our meeting but never had an occasion to tell anyone about one of my dreams, until...

The day was a typical surgical mix of emergencies and consults with not enough time to finish one problem when another appeared. I was tired when I got home and went to bed earlier than usual, but my sleep was interrupted by a strong, frightening emotion. My stomach was in knots from the most vivid dream of my life. I was watching myself in line at a funeral home, exchanging conversation with many friends. Flower arrangements lined the walls, and quiet classical music played in the background. Many were crying as they passed the open coffin holding the body of my best friend, Judge Mike Glasso. In my dream, he died suddenly, in his fifties, leaving stunned family, friends, and colleagues.

The judge, starting from humble beginnings in a working-class family, achieved great success in his life. The turning point came in high school, when he was chastised by the assistant dean of boys for not living up to his great potential. The dean sat down with him and gave him this sobering advice, "Shape up or ship out. You should really quit school and get a job since you will never amount to anything." That was just the reverse psychology Mike needed, and he became a student on a mission to prove the dean wrong.

Mike graduated from high school and was only the second person in his family to enter college. There he was influenced by a professor to study law. Realizing that professional school would give him a greater chance to help others, he put himself through Chicago-Kent Law School by selling shoes. He was the valedictorian in his class, and, in his graduation speech, he encouraged his fellow students to do "good things" as lawyers. That became the motto for his life. He developed a program utilizing clinical psychologists to help the courts determine the best interests of the children in divorce proceedings. His model was adopted by the State of Illinois and many other states.

Wishing to have an even greater impact, he progressed from county judge to chief judge and, ultimately, to one of a select group of Illinois Appellate judges. Now in my dream, his life was prematurely over from an acute heart attack. His face, retouched with funeral makeup, appeared as clear as in real life. I was totally overcome with emotion.

The next morning, I went through my work on autopilot with an ache that would not leave my chest. I remembered Janet's advice about revealing your dream to friends, but I struggled with how to tell my best friend that I saw his body in a funeral home. I finally resolved to call as soon as I finished my day.

That evening I sat by the phone for several minutes contemplating the words I would use to express myself without emotion. This would be hard. I reached for the phone. I had the script arranged in my mind. My hand was sweating as I listened to the mechanical ring tone. Then he answered.

"Mike," I said, "I had a dream about you last night and felt I had to tell you about it."

"Okay," he said.

"This is hard for me to say, but I dreamed that you were dead, and I saw you lying in a casket in a funeral home."

Mike laughed. "That was some dream," he said, still laughing.

As I told him more of the details he stopped laughing. I think he realized how upset I was.

"Would you just do me a favor, and get a physical?" I asked.

"Sure," he said. "If you think it's important, I'll do it for you. I haven't had a physical for a while anyway."

I took a deep breath. I had done my job, and if there was a heart problem, his doctor would find it.

Life went back to normal, and it was two weeks before we spoke on the phone again.

"Hello, Rich," he said. "Well, I had my physical, and everything was just fine. I'm glad your dream was not prophetic. I had the blood tests, an EKG, and an X-ray, and he told me I was in perfect health. In fact, my internist said that I shouldn't listen to my friends about my health, and I could stop worrying about dying."

I didn't know how to respond, because I suddenly got that sick feeling all over again. I thanked him for the update, but over the next several days I could not get him off my mind. The dream was too real to ignore, so I called him back. "Mike, would you consider doing one more test, an ultrafast heart scan that can give an indication of whether your coronary arteries are blocked?"

He hesitated. "Do you think I *really* need to?" he asked.

"It would make me feel better," I said, still remembering his ghostly face in my dream. I was going out on a limb and would be embarrassed if things were perfectly normal, but that little voice in the back of my head was too strong to ignore. If I was wrong, we were good enough friends that he would forgive me. After some hesitation, he finally agreed. Another sigh of relief!

Judge Mike made that appointment for the heart scan, and it was so abnormal that his cardiologists, Dr. Rauh and Dr. Kerwin, scheduled an urgent angiogram (catheter study with dye to visualize the arteries in the heart). I canceled my morning appointments so I could be with my good friend on the morning of his procedure.

Mike and I spoke inside his room before his angiogram about how unusual it would be for anything serious to be found since he had shown no symptoms at all. When he was called to the cath lab, I walked beside his gurney until he was taken into the procedure room. We were both anxious, but I think I was more concerned, because it was my insistence that brought him to this point. The procedure went well, and when it was over, Dr. Kerwin opened the door and signaled for me to come inside. We looked at the films together. Without speaking, he pointed to two of the three main arteries of the heart, which were 90 percent blocked. In addition, the main trunk was also partially blocked, a condition called the "widow maker."

"It's surprising he is still alive!" said Dr. Kerwin.

He called Bob Angelos, the cardiac surgeon, who put Mike on the schedule for bypass the following day. He was afraid that if he waited any longer, the judge might have a fatal heart attack. This much coronary disease, if untreated, usually results in death within months.

Judge Mike was sedated but not out of earshot of our conversation. He motioned for me to come to his side, and, with a voice trembling with emotion, whispered, "Rich, thanks... thanks for saving my life! I guess you and God were looking out for me."

I was humbled with emotion as Mike's words made me realize that I had been the messenger in God's hands.

Judge Mike underwent an uneventful cardiac bypass procedure and was out of the hospital in four days and back to the courtroom in six weeks. When he finally retired and moved to Florida, he left behind a legacy that touched the lives of countless children and families. That was fifteen years and a thousand golf games ago, many played with me.

And, no, thankfully, I haven't had any more dreams about friends.

CHAPTER 16

OPERATING IN THE PHILIPPINES

~

MICHAEL I. HUSSEY, MD

I WAS IN TROUBLE, AND I knew it. Marie's surgery had been routine until she was suddenly bleeding uncontrollably from multiple sites. To complicate the problem, I was the only surgeon in the tiny eight-bed rural hospital, and the blood bank was twenty miles away.

It was our traditional February mission trip to one of the outer islands of the Philippines. I had been richly blessed to achieve my dream of becoming a surgeon, and this was my way of giving back, at least partially. The Catholic mission in charge of our agenda believed in sending us to the poorest locations in the world where our skills and knowledge could do the greatest good, and, on this trip, they divided the thirty physicians and allied medical personnel into two work groups. When we left Chicago, it was cold and snowing, but here in the tropics, our daily temperature was between seventy and eighty degrees.

Our group was taken from the main airport to a relatively modern city, Bacolod, where we stayed in a Western-style hotel. However, every morning we were transported back in time, traveling in a vintage bus to a rural hospital where the practice of medicine and surgery had not progressed beyond the 1950s. On the way, we passed through some of the most lush and beautiful scenery in the world, with tropical bamboo forests bordering rich farm fields of sugarcane and rice. The road was paved but so infrequently traveled that tropical vegetation grew in all the cracks, and farmers used the road to dry their rice. The bus driver navigated around each rice mound without a second thought.

When we arrived at the hospital, I was not surprised to see a two-story edifice with peeling paint and rusty metal supports. It had the capacity for twenty beds, but the second floor was unused, making it an eight-bed hospital primarily for trauma from automobile accidents. Considering what I observed about the Philippine driving habits, this must have been a great need. When I saw the two marginally equipped operating rooms, I was thankful that I brought a bag from home containing over thirty pounds of scalpels, suture material, retractors, clamps, needles, and syringes.

If greater operating capacity was needed, they simply set up two tables in one room. It was not uncommon for the lights to go out in the middle of a case, but there was no panic. The staff simply moved the operating table near the window, and the surgery continued as if nothing had happened. We found to our amazement that even under such primitive conditions, our surgical outcomes were as good as in our modern hospitals back home, but I still wonder if there was something more than good fortune behind those results.

All of the Philippine people who were suffering, including the affluent, wanted to see the "American" doctors, but the mission prearranged clinic visits only for the indigent who could not afford medical care. On my first few trips, I expected to find that the people would be depressed over their lot in life, but I found just the opposite. Even the poorest of the poor were smiling, sometimes without teeth, and a billboard next to the road leading to our city featured two joyful girls with the caption, "Welcome to the city of smiles."

The humble Philippine people expressed great appreciation for what we were doing and brought us gifts of food and handcrafted presents whenever they could. On our first day, we were honored with a traditional feast of roasted pig. One of the delicacies they reserved for special guests was the cooked fatty skin. I thought it looked like whale blubber, but I ate as much as I could tolerate to avoid offending our hosts.

After our welcoming dinner, I asked to tour where our patients lived. I was taken down a country road to what looked like a slum with hundreds and possibly thousands of houses built on stilts with cardboard or tin siding. "Why were they built above ground?" I asked our guide.

"There is no sanitary system, and all the sewage goes directly onto the ground," he replied.

"I think I would want my home to be on stilts too," I said.

With my obstetrics and gynecology specialty, most of my surgeries were for pelvic tumors and bleeding. On our first clinic day, patients lined up for blocks. Their conditions always seemed to be the extreme of what I was used to seeing. With little medical care, they had to wait for a foreign medical team to arrive before they could have their procedures, and our trip was usually life changing for them (and often for us too). When it was time to return home, I always wanted to stay to help the women who would have to wait a year before they could have their surgeries, and we all knew some would not survive until the next year.

Marie was one of the patients who waited in line for hours on my first clinic day. She had a natural beauty, with long, straight dark hair and a shy smile, but she was so desperately poor that she could not afford to see a physician. She was a diligent mother who loved and cared for her family despite suffering from a chronically distended abdomen and intractable pain.

As I examined her, I confirmed that she had a large mass in her pelvis. Without an ultrasound, I could not determine at the time if it was cancer or a benign tumor, but it turned out that Marie suffered from a large benign fibroid uterus. This was one of the largest I had ever seen, being at least the size of a small watermelon. We scheduled her for surgery the coming week.

I was the only gynecologist and often the only surgeon in our small outlying hospital. The other physicians were assigned to a different island two hundred miles away. When I started Marie's surgery, I did not even have a scrub nurse to assist, only some willing but inexperienced Philippine technicians. I thought about all the amenities I took for granted back in the States. We had access to a pharmacy that would deliver drugs immediately to the operating room. Here, we would either not have the medication or would need to get it ourselves. The instruments were ones I remembered using in my early training in the 1960s.

Marie's surgery started uneventfully with a midline incision, but as I began to explore her abdomen, I found more than I expected. In addition to the large fibroid tumors in her uterus, she also had multiple ovarian cysts. Then everything was matted together with scar tissue from years and years of untreated endometriosis (a condition where parts of the uterine tissue spread throughout the abdomen). We call this a "frozen pelvis," because everything looks like it is frozen together in one large mass, and it prevents access to the major feeding blood vessels behind the uterus that need to be tied off to prevent excessive bleeding.

As I contemplated what to do next, Marie's surgical sites started to ooze. At first it was not serious, and I kept control with cautery, but then more areas opened up, and I found myself working faster and faster to control each bleeder. I looked at my first tech assistant and I could see in his eyes that he shared my concern. I knew he was relying on me to come up with a solution.

Instinctively, I leaned over to ask for some blood from the blood bank until I remembered the blood bank was twenty miles away. By this time, the bleeding was filling her abdomen. Here I was, the only surgeon in a rural hospital, thousands of miles from home, with little trained help, operating on a young woman whose bleeding was out of control.

I started mentally calculating how much time I would have before she literally bled to death. I could not get to the source of the bleeding and could not work fast enough to forestall the impending disaster unfolding before my eyes. My surgical assistants stopped talking, and the room fell into an eerie silence.

I looked back at Marie's peaceful sleeping face. She had no idea that her fate was now uncertain. As she became paler and paler, I knew I needed a miracle to save her life.

I closed my eyes and quietly whispered, "God, I am your instrument, and you are the healer. This is your patient. Please take over. Amen."

I opened my eyes to the bright surgical light to witness something beyond explanation. The tissue planes that were obliterated by scar tissue had fallen open, allowing me to reach the major blood vessels behind the uterus. Quickly I tied off each one. The bleeding stopped! I stood for a minute, trying to contemplate what had just happened. I looked again at my surgical assistants and could imagine the smiles behind their surgical masks. I'm sure they thought I had just performed something incredible.

They were correct. It was incredible. I had never experienced anything like this before, but I believe that afternoon in a tiny insignificant hospital in a rural part of the Philippines, I simply became the first assistant—to an eternal Surgeon.

Marie went to recovery, and then to her room, in stable condition. The rest of the afternoon was spent on autopilot. I had trouble concentrating after witnessing what had just taken place. The next morning on rounds, I spoke with Marie through our translator.

"How do you feel?" I asked.

"Tired but wonderful," she said. "Thank you for performing such a great work for me."

"Yesterday, I was just the servant," I said. "The work was done by our Heavenly Father, who saved your life when He took over in the operating room."

Marie smiled. She continued to recover and was able to leave the hospital for a normal life with her family.

Some months later I received this grateful note which read, in effect,

Dear Dr. Hussey,

Thank you for helping me. I am doing well.

Marie

I remembered using those same words in the operating room after her surgery when I bowed my head and prayed, *"Dear Heavenly Father, thank You for helping me."*

I was also doing well.

CHAPTER 17

TROUBLE ON THE MOUNTAIN

~

STEPHEN E. HEIM, MD

IT WAS A PERFECT DAY in the mountains of Keystone, Colorado. The snow was deep and powdery, and with the reflection of the sun off the slopes, I had to squint as I walked out the condominium door. I was looking forward to a long weekend of skiing. It had been a busy two weeks trying to get away from my orthopedic spine practice. I think everyone had to see me before I left. The phone never stopped ringing, and I was late getting out of the office. This always happens when I plan a vacation. I usually pack last minute, and this trip was no exception.

My wife and her sister were getting their equipment together. The air was crisp as we walked to the first lift. We were all experienced skiers and headed for the more difficult black diamond runs. As we approached the top of the lift, my eyes were drawn to a more remote mountain. It held my attention in an unusual and mysterious way. We would try that run in the afternoon, but I never dreamed that my experience on that mountain would change my life.

Our morning of skiing was exhilarating and tiring. We took a break for lunch in the village. Then we were ready for the new mountain and a new challenge. Every run was a black diamond, and from the rugged and steep rock formations, I could see why. As we approached the lift, the sky clouded over, and snow began to fall. It was gentle at first, and then became heavier. As we reached the top of the lift, the wind was howling, and the temperature dropped. We were now in a full-blown blizzard on an unfamiliar mountain with only one way down. I took out the map and held it tightly so it wouldn't be blown out of my hands. The visibility was only thirty feet, so I studied the run carefully to make sure we wouldn't become lost. Finally I yelled, "Let's go!"

The first part of the run was steep, and I had all I could do to keep an eye on where I was going and still try to stay with the women. Suddenly, an island of trees appeared in front of us, and we had to go either left or right. I chose the right fork, but as soon as I did, I realized I was on the "path less taken." My wife and her sister and most of the other skiers went to the left. I could tell from the direction I was going that within a few seconds we would be widely separated in an evolving mountain blizzard. I could do only one thing; I turned my skis and headed into the forest to rejoin my party. The snow in the wooded area was not packed down, so I knew that I needed to keep my momentum. If I stopped, I would not be able to restart in such deep powder.

The wind whistled down the run, but there was an eerie silence in the woods. I had a foreboding feeling in my chest, like I was being summoned to participate in a struggle of life-and-death proportions. I stopped. As I sank down, chest deep in the snow, I looked around and could see nothing but trees. I took off my skis and paused for a moment to try to understand what I was doing. My brain told me that I should hurry to get back to the main path, but some indescribable urge directed me to climb back up the mountain. This was not the direction that would lead me back. I knew that. The mountain was steep, and climbing was difficult in chest-deep snow, but the air had become so unusually calm that I could hear the crunch of my boots and the sound of my heavy breathing.

After twenty agonizing yards, I came to a large pine tree. I looked down and realized why I was there. Lying deep in the tree well was the mangled shape of a body, completely covered with snow. If I were not standing immediately next to the tree, it would have been totally invisible. I brushed the snow off a lifeless gray face. He looked dead, but I instinctively reached down to feel for a carotid artery pulse. His skin was cold from hypothermia.

A chill came over my body, not from the cold, but from the realization that this was a déjà vu experience. This was exactly what happened to me two years before, but that time the victim was not a total stranger, but my father!

We were cross-country skiing in the Upper Peninsula of Michigan. An expert skier, my father joined me on trails that were being used for training by the US and German Olympic teams. We had been out only a short time when a sudden storm blew in off Lake Superior. The snow came down so hard that visibility was minimal, and the temperature dropped to fifteen degrees below zero, with a wind chill considerably below that. The German skiers told us that an emergency weather alert had sounded, and they were called off the course. My father decided to rest on one of the higher trails, while my mother and I were farther down. When we heard the alert, I hurried back to meet him.

He was lying in the snow when I arrived, ashen in color and gripping his chest. Knowing immediately that he was having a heart attack, I got out my cell phone and was fortunately able to call the paramedics at the lodge. My father was panting heavily. He looked terrible. Within minutes, a snowmobile arrived, and we administered nitroglycerine under his tongue, relieving his chest pain by opening the arteries in his heart. My father perked up, and some of his color returned, but I knew I had to get him to help immediately. It would take about forty-five minutes to get from that location to the nearest emergency room, since the ambulance needed to drive around the entire mountain. A clinic was just over a mile from where we were, and I could run there in fifteen minutes. The paramedics were evidently only authorized to take us back to the lodge and waiting ambulance and not to the clinic. My heart started to pound. I knew what I had to do.

I picked my father up in my arms, moved him to my back, and ran. I work out with cardio and weights nearly every day, but I knew this would be my supreme test. I had to get my father to the emergency clinic immediately. I could feel my adrenalin flow, and his limp, two hundred pound body did not seem heavy at all. Everything moved in slow motion. I knew exactly where to run, around the side of the mountain, through the woods, and down to the clinic where the emergency physician was on duty. He and I both trained at Northwestern University.

I had been running for about fifteen minutes when I caught sight of the smoke coming from the clinic chimney. My father groaned, and, as I turned my head to look, he was blue again. I couldn't feel a pulse, so I began to sprint. I had to get him there fast. Those last thirty seconds were the longest of my life.

I burst through the door of the clinic and into the treatment room, put my father down on the exam table, stripped off his jacket, and immediately started CPR. My doctor colleague recognized exactly what was happening and grabbed the defibrillator paddles. "Clear," he said as he administered the first shock to his chest.

My father's rhythm was ventricular fibrillation, a fatal rhythm from an acute heart attack. He remained unconscious as we continued to do CPR. My friend, Dr. Roberts, was a well-trained emergency physician, and he knew all the right IV drugs to administer along with a periodic shock to help convert the heart to a regular rhythm. We traded off doing CPR. I was drenched in sweat. We worked for another hour, and, despite doing everything right, his rhythm degenerated into a flat line. Dr. Roberts looked at me. There were tears in my eyes. We both knew the outcome.

He was gone. Nothing we could do would bring him back. I had done everything right. We were both experts in trauma medicine. We called the code, and I sat down and sobbed. There was nothing more we could do.

Why did this have to happen to me? I was used to saving lives, not losing them.

I shook my head and brought my mind back to the stranger lying under the tree. He looked just like my father had. I positioned my hand over his carotid artery—although it was very weak, there was a pulse. Was this God's way of giving me a second chance?

Like two years before, everything started to move in slow motion. From my experience as a trauma surgeon and working as a physician with the Navy, I knew what to do. I stripped off my outer clothes and, after brushing the snow off, covered his body with my warm clothing. I moved him into a position where his head was down and feet up (called reverse Trendelenburg) to allow as much blood to get to his brain as possible. His lower leg was at a ninety-degree angle, so I quickly pulled off a lower pine branch, stripped the twigs, and splinted his leg in a straight position. I was doing everything at once, all the time yelling at the top of my lungs, "*Help; help; help!*"

Was I too far into the woods for anyone to hear me? I checked his pulse again. It was still weak and thready, but he was alive. Should I pick him up and run? The snow was too deep and the mountain too treacherous. I yelled again, "*Help; help; help!*" Even though the air was getting colder and colder, I felt comfortable without my jacket on. Over and over in my mind I kept wondering what I would do if no one heard my desperate plea.

Suddenly a snow-covered head peered out from behind the tree. "Can I help?" he asked.

"Yes. Get to an emergency phone along the ski run and call the snow patrol. He's almost dead. Hurry!"

My unknown friend rushed off, making his way through deep snow back to the run, and then down the slope to the nearest emergency phone.

I stood like a sentinel near the pine tree, watching both for the lights of the ski patrol and to make sure my victim was still breathing. Would I be able to save him? My mind continued to flash back to my father. My emotion was so strong that tears welled up in my eyes. I knew that this was my second chance and that someone above had directed me here, not only to save this man's life but also my own.

Then I heard the faint sound of the snowmobile and saw the lights. They seemed to know where to go and were next to me in no time. I helped them lift my limp victim onto the stretcher, and they sped off to a waiting ambulance at the lodge. I put my vest and jacket back on, and suddenly I realized just how cold it really was. I shivered uncontrollably. It must have been forty below with the wind chill. I hiked out of the woods as quickly as I could and found the trail. To my surprise, my wife and her sister were huddled together waiting for me. It was too cold to tell them the whole story, so we quickly skied down to the lodge.

For my efforts, the ski patrol left a certificate good for a free cup of hot chocolate. I smiled. By this time I was trembling from my post adrenaline rush.

That night we celebrated with a large steak dinner and a bottle of wine. The next day, I went to the ski patrol station and enquired about my stranger. He was taken to a local hospital where he not only survived, but was up and talking that morning. He had suffered from hypothermia and a broken leg, but the orthopedist on the case was impressed with my splinting. The only other information they provided was that he was a plumbing contractor from Colorado.

There was no question in my mind that I had been directed to a stranger who suffered a concussion after striking a tree, and if I had not come right up to the tree, no one would have found him until the snow melted in the spring.

But the greatest lesson I learned that day was my own. I had been carrying the burden of my father's death for two years, feeling that if I had only done more, he would have survived. I could now accept the fact that there is a higher power that determines life and death, and that his time had come. Having the chance to save a stranger in trouble was God's way of giving me a second chance, and I passed. I think my dad may have been in on the plan.

Thanks, Dad.

CHAPTER 18

SHOPPING FOR A MIRACLE

~

GORDON D. BROWN, MD

Dear Dr. Brown,

I just wanted to write you and thank you for your provi-dential care while in the hospital, as well as let you know about my recovery.

First and foremost, I am back to being a full-time wife and mother. I am also back to all the activities I have previously enjoyed: running, biking, playing ball, hiking, etc.

I have felt strongly that you were the direct link in my marvelous recovery from paralysis or worse. Thank you for the life you have lived that has allowed you to be led by our Father in heaven. My life will be forever changed because of Dr. Gordon Brown.

Gratefully,
Mandy Blake

I will never forget Mandy. She was a vibrant and exciting young woman with a smile that would melt your heart. She was admitted to the Provo, Utah, hospital for the delivery of their second child. I have treasured her thank-you note because it reminds me of the miracle that happened to both of us that eventful spring day.

Her story started with an uncomplicated delivery of a healthy young son. She was discharged home but returned just over two weeks later with a swollen, painful left leg. Her obstetrician ordered an ultrasound to screen for blood clots.

The test was positive for an extensive blood clot in the major veins in her leg, and a subsequent study confirmed a clot that extended into her pelvis. The usual treatment for this is to start a blood thinner, like heparin, to prevent further clotting while the body dissolves the clot. However, the block was so extensive that if we simply did the standard treatment, the vein would never open fully, and she would be left with a chronically swollen and uncomfortable leg.

As an interventional radiologist, I was called to put a catheter into the vein that was clotted and infuse a specialized clot dissolver to help open the vein permanently. There is some risk in doing this because the medication we use (TPA) is so powerful that there is a chance of a hemorrhage developing somewhere else in the body. However, we spoke with the obstetrician, Mandy, and her family and felt that it was reasonably safe to proceed.

The catheter was placed without complication, and the infusion started. This usually lasts for two to three days depending upon how well the clot is dissolving. The first two days went well, and we decided to continue a third day to see if we could fully open the vein and relieve the painful swelling in her leg. She was in good spirits when I saw her that morning for rounds.

This was my day off, and, after rounds, I went shopping in Salt Lake City, an hour away. Most of the time, a doctor's day off is really not a day off, since we may be called in for an emergency or have an endless stack of paperwork to complete. But I was careful this day to clear my schedule to do some much-needed shopping.

The weather was beautiful as I drove to Salt Lake and started at my favorite mall. At about two o'clock, I felt an uneasy sense of foreboding. It was a strange feeling I could not fully explain. My thoughts turned to Mandy, and I wondered how she was doing. In between stores, I called the hospital and spoke with her nurse.

"She is doing just fine, Dr. Brown," her nurse told me.

"Let's stop her TPA infusion," I said. "I feel uneasy about continuing. I think she has had enough."

I continued my shopping, but my mind was just not in it. I kept thinking about Mandy. The feeling grew progressively stronger and more unsettling. I wanted to relax and enjoy the day, but I could not. Finally, at around three o'clock, I knew I needed to stop and immediately go back to the hospital. My mind was focused on getting back as quickly as I could, and I was speeding as I traveled the hour back to Provo.

When I got to the hospital, I ran up the stairs and right to Mandy's room.

"Are you okay?" I asked.

"I'm having some trouble moving my left leg," she said. "And my right leg is becoming numb also."

I did a quick neurologic exam and found that her left leg was partially paralyzed, and there was some weakness now in the right leg. I called down to radiology to inform them that we needed an emergency MRI. I also called my friend, Dr. Nelson, an outstanding neurosurgeon.

"I need you right away," I said. "I have a maternity patient who I think has bled around her spine and may need emergency surgery." Fortunately, he was in the hospital and said he would meet me in radiology.

The MRI scanner was open, and her nurse and I wheeled Mandy down to the radiology department. I waited in the control room as the pictures came out on the screen. It was just what I suspected: a hemorrhage in her lower back was causing pressure on the spinal nerves, with resulting paralysis. This was truly a medical emergency. If not corrected immediately, the paralysis and loss of bowel and bladder control would be permanent.

My palms were sweating as Dr. Nelson entered the control room and looked at the images.

"You were right," he said. "This will need emergency evacuation."

We were in the operating room within thirty minutes. Dr. Nelson and I both scrubbed and gowned and proceeded with the surgery. He was able to evacuate the collection of blood surrounding her spinal canal without complication. Fortunately, because I had stopped the infusion of blood thinner at two o'clock, Dr. Nelson was able to control all the bleeding and finish the operation.

I saw Mandy in the recovery room, and she was already able to move her left leg. I met with her husband and expressed optimism that she would recover.

That night was one of the longest of my life. I woke up early and went into the hospital. What I found the next morning was a smiling new mother with marked improvement in the function of her legs. That was a great moment for me. A few days later, she walked out of the hospital with her baby in her arms and no residual paralysis at all.

Before she left, Mandy asked me to sit down. With a tear in her eye, she asked why I knew to come back to save her from a life confined to a wheelchair. My only explanation was that God saved two people that day, a beautiful young mother and a caring physician who felt responsible for her life.

Mandy and her family are doing well to this day.

And yes, Mrs. Brown, I'm still wearing that worn jacket I know I need to replace on my next shopping trip—someday.

CHAPTER 19

THE LUNCH MEETING

~ঽ

KEVIN RUSSEAU, DC

AS THE NEW CHIROPRACTOR IN town, I was nervous about building up clientele. After all, I needed to pay the bills. So I was excited to receive an invitation to a meeting of local professionals that had the networking potential to launch my practice to the next level. What an amazing opportunity! When the day finally came, my palms were damp as I walked into the plush red banquet room filled with *the* local professional movers and shakers.

I was seated next to John Robertson, a crisis intervention specialist. After the leadership introductions and a prayer, we had a polite conversation over lunch. When we finished our meal, I stood up to get to my "real" purpose of the meeting, networking. As I excused myself, John looked directly at me and, in a quiet, unassuming manner, invited me to sit for a minute longer to listen to a story he felt I needed to hear. His sincere expression and gentle smile held a magnetism that I simply could not refuse, so I settled back into my chair to listen.

"When I was younger and learning my profession," he told me, "I received a call on the crisis line from a young lady who said she was calling just to talk to someone. I let her talk about her life for an extended time. She denied that she was depressed, but as we spoke, I kept getting the distinct impression that she needed to be hospitalized. The feeling grew stronger and stronger, and I finally revealed my impressions to her. As I did, she broke down in tears and admitted that she was planning to commit suicide. Because of the bond that developed during our conversation, she agreed to go to the closest emergency room for help. I checked on her later that day and found that she was admitted to our community hospital psychiatric unit and ultimately recovered and was discharged."

As John related his story, his face became animated with a passion for his work that I had never seen in anyone before. I was on the edge of my seat during his captivating story. He told me how he recognized the severity of the problem and how he was able to defuse the immediate crisis. He acted on feelings and instincts, not facts alone.

As he finished, I saw people getting up to leave. The meeting was over. To my dismay, I realized I had lost the opportunity to accomplish any networking. John's story, while riveting, would never benefit my practice.

At one thirty, I was back at the office seeing patients. This was one of my long days, and my last appointment was at seven o'clock. By that time I was always very tired and hungry. My last patient was Tim Johnson, a laborer who hurt his back on the job. I sensed that there was something unusual in our interaction, but I completed his intake and started the treatment for his significant back injury. By the time I finished and picked up the office, it was after eight.

I locked the door, but as my hand reached to turn off the lights, it stopped in midair. Suddenly and inexplicably, I felt the need to call Tim Johnson, my last patient. I knew dinner was on the table waiting for me, but I walked back to my desk, picked up the phone, and dialed his number. Tim answered, and I told him I felt I needed to follow up. After an uncomfortable pause, he opened up. He had been struggling with depression and was unhappy with his life. Since I spent my lunch that day with a social worker who specialized in depression, I asked Tim if I could make his introduction. He agreed, and we hung up so I could make the connection.

Thankfully, John Robertson's card was right on my desk in front of me. I was a little surprised that I had kept it, since I usually toss calling cards I would not place in my Rolodex.

I dialed his office number, expecting to leave a message but was surprised when he personally answered. He had been working late and was just leaving when I phoned. I related the information about my new patient. When we hung up, I called Tim back with the information, and then went home for dinner, satisfied that I had done what that little voice in the back of my head was telling me to do. Fortunately the events of that long disappointing day would soon be lost in the din of work and life.

About six months later, during a typical office day, I discovered that Tim Johnson was in an exam room waiting to see me. I walked in with a smile and offered to shake his hand, but Tim suddenly broke down and cried uncontrollably. I went over to comfort him, but it was a long time before he was composed enough to tell me his emotional story.

"When I saw you six months ago," he said, "I was in the depths of a depression and planned to go home and take my life. I had everything ready, but your call literally stopped me. When I spoke with Mr. Robertson, your crisis worker, he was able to recognize my desperation and calmly convinced me to go to the emergency room. I was admitted to the psychiatric crisis center where counseling and medication turned my life around. I now have a new job where I don't have to use my back. That's why I haven't needed to see you. My life is good; in fact, it's great! Thank you. Thank you so much for saving my life!"

Now we were both crying. What I thought had been an unproductive, forgettable day turned out to be a day I would remember forever. Spending my lunch being educated by a crisis social worker, using my new knowledge to recognize a serious depression, and acting on my feelings to catch John Robertson unexpectedly in his office were all part of a finely orchestrated plan. The real purpose of my "networking" meeting was not about networking at all, but about saving a life. The healer in me was humbled by the knowledge that I was directed that day by the wisdom of none other than the Master Healer.

CHAPTER 20

A FRIEND IN TROUBLE

~

DOUGLAS JOHNSON, MD, PHD

I ATTENDED A CONFERENCE IN Ohio on the latest develop-
ments in the treatment of stroke, and one lecture held a
strange fascination for me about research on a new technique
for opening clotted arteries in the brain. I attend three or
four medical conferences a year and initially did not believe
my urgency to attend this particular meeting was anything
out of the ordinary, until a few weeks later when I was called to
the emergency room to consult on one of my own colleagues,
Dr. Andrew Reagan.

Andy was a neurosurgical friend who injured his neck in
a skiing accident during a trip to British Columbia. After his
return, his first symptoms were shoulder pain, nausea, and
lightheadedness while he was seeing patients in his office.
His nurse checked his blood pressure, which was dangerously
low. He refused to go to the emergency department, thinking, like many doctors, that he was bulletproof and indestruc-
tible. Instead his wife brought him home, where he developed
slurred speech, and then weakness on his left side.

Soon Andy's home was filled with concerned practitioners, including his neurosurgical partner, his physician assistant, and a neurologist who recognized the severity of the problem and called 911. Just as the ambulance arrived, Andy's eyes rolled back, and he went into full cardiac arrest. The paramedics started CPR and quickly transported him to the local emergency department, where his heart came back into a normal rhythm, but he was only intermittently conscious.

When I arrived in the ER to see my patient, it was an emotionally charged visit, finding a friend lying on a gurney under bright lights, unable to communicate. I felt a hollow feeling in my chest when I reviewed his brain scans, which revealed his terminal diagnosis, a clotted basilar artery supplying blood to the back of the brain and the brain stem. These are vital areas for life, and there was no current treatment for these clots. I felt the anguish of knowing I could do nothing to alter his impending death spiral, as his brain would continue to swell until it ultimately extinguished his life.

As I reviewed the films a second time, searching for some ray of hope, I remembered what I had learned in Ohio several weeks before about dissolving this exact type of clot and wished we had that capability.

I slowly walked to the physician consultation room where his wife was waiting. This would be a tough conversation, and I dreaded giving her the news. In my mind, I kept going over and over what words I could say that would provide any comfort at all. Then I abruptly stopped walking as a thought flashed through my mind. What if we *could* dissolve that clot? Could I pull this off? There had to be a way!

Now I was trembling as I entered the room. His wife, Joan, was pacing and beside herself with concern. "Please sit down," I told her. "I'm so sorry about Andy. If we do nothing, he will not survive. And even if we do something, his chance of making it is still very small. He has clotted the major artery supplying the back of the brain and the brain stem. I attended a conference several weeks ago, and one of the presentations was on dissolving clotted arteries like his. It has only been done at two research centers in the country, but with your permission, I would like to try to do it here."

After composing herself, she said, "Yes, yes, please do everything you can."

I had never done anything like this before, and was now a little anxious about what I had promised I could do. My first call was to the neurologist who made the conference presentation. It took multiple calls to his office, hospital, and finally home before I was able to reach him. He refused to give me the details of the procedure because it was not FDA approved, and if there was a serious complication, we could all be in legal trouble. I didn't know what to say, so I simply explained Andy's desperate situation. When I finished, there was a very uncomfortable silence. I knew I had to let him speak first if I had any chance of gaining his support.

Finally, he said, "What's your fax number?"

I did it! But I also knew that this was just the first in a series of approvals that would be needed before we could do what was a very radical procedure at the time.

My cardiology friends, who were familiar with TPA for heart arteries, were an easy sell. They were anxious to try something they had never seen attempted before. My next hurdle was to speak with the hospital administrator, attorney, and hospital board. They would all need to authorize this unapproved procedure. While they deliberated on this literal life-and-death decision, Andy was slowly slipping away.

It was late in the evening, and I was still at the hospital when I received this call from the hospital administrator. "We are willing to take the risk to potentially save a life," she said.

I almost cried with relief. I called Beth, my wife, and told her I would not be home until the early hours of the morning. Accustomed to my erratic schedule, she graciously wished me luck.

My cardiology team now rushed back to the hospital while Andy was escorted to the cath lab (where angiograms are done). His wife, tightly holding his hand, remained at his side with trembling words of comfort to a husband whose life expectancy was measured in hours.

In the lab, the cardiologists meticulously threaded the catheter to the origin of the basilar artery and started the infusion of the blood-thinning TPA using the formula I provided. I watched the monitor expectantly, but nothing happened, except a complication. He started to bleed from multiple sites including his IV, mouth, and even a tear in his eye turned red! We controlled the bleeding sites with pressure and continued to wait for any neurologic change. Nothing! Instead, he slipped into a deep coma.

Disappointed and frustrated, I was resigned that I had done all that I could do. We transferred Andy to the ICU, and I went home exhausted, hoping to catch a few hours of sleep before morning rounds.

The next day, Andy remained unresponsive on full life support. When I met with his wife, I told her that I was devastated that Andy showed no signs of improvement, but we agreed to keep him on the ventilator for one more day. When the second morning dawned with no change, I felt that our procedure had failed. My conclusion was shared by his neurologist, who told Joan that Andy had no brain activity and recommended he be taken off the ventilator and allowed to die. His wife was not emotionally ready to withdraw life support, however, so we agreed to postpone the decision until the next day.

On the third morning, I met with the family first. Everyone was crying, but our meeting was interrupted by one of the nurses in the unit who excitedly reported that she had witnessed some eyelid movement. I went in to examine him, moved close to his ear, and said in a loud voice, "Andy, if you can hear me, blink your eyes three times." There was a flutter of his eyelids. It happened so quickly that I stepped back in surprise. To make sure it really happened, I said again, "Andy, you had a serious stroke and may never be the same again. If you don't want us to remove life support, blink three times."

What happened then is something I will remember the rest of my life. He started to blink and he kept blinking and blinking and blinking and blinking. What an unbelievable sign. A broad smile appeared on my face that I could not suppress!

Over the next few days Andy's blinking turned into a complex code for spelling out words from an alphabet board with one blink down, two over to the right, and so on. Then, one morning when it was clear that he was going to survive, came this short but unforgettable message:

"D-O-U-G T-H-A-N-K-S F-O-R M-Y L-I-F-E"

I wiped away a tear. The TPA had worked, his blood flow was restored to his brain, and he was coming back.

Andy was transferred to a rehabilitation hospital for his prolonged recovery, and he eventually regained all of his faculties. After discharge, he made the decision to retire because his arms and legs were not strong enough to permit delicate neurosurgical procedures. He moved to Florida, where he continues to help others in his new callings in his church and community.

As a younger man, I thought that my experience with Andy was just a series of coincidences, but with the perspective of age, I know that was not the case. What I felt that night was an invisible force guiding my actions to save a friend in trouble, and strengthening my faith to face my own eternal journey.*

---

* *Dr. Johnson lost his battle with cancer and died shortly after this story was completed.*

CHAPTER 21

FAMILY CONNECTIONS

∼

ANONYMOUS, MD

I PICKED UP THE PHONE on the kitchen table to renew my prescriptions online, but I could not coordinate my fingers with my brain. After three attempts, I stopped trying. I'm surprised now that I was not more concerned. I just thought it might get better if I waited. When my left arm, left face, and left leg started to tingle, I should have recognized that I was having a stroke. Whether it was denial or mental fog that prevented me from calling for help, I'm not sure. I am very familiar with the clot-dissolving drugs used in the emergency department that can reverse stroke paralysis and prevent the death of the millions of brain cells that are lost every minute. I simply lacked the energy to do anything but sit there. And that's what I did until I was startled by the sudden chirp of a text message from my sister, April.

I have two sisters, April and Beth. Our family is very close and has always been connected in unusual ways. I remember driving home in rush hour when I was in my anesthesia residency in Boston. My mind wandered as I inched along on Highway 9 west of town, watching the brake lights flash on and off. I kept thinking about my sister's new baby, Jessica, born six months before, the pride of the family and the first child of the next generation. I wondered what our family would do if something happened to my sister Beth and her husband, Frank. I loved little Jessica like my own, so it was an easy transition to conclude that my wife and I would adopt her. That would make sense, and it gave me a warm, comfortable feeling inside to come to that mental decision, as if I were answering a request from her mother.

My thoughts nicely occupied most of the rush hour, and I soon found myself pulling into the parking space of our apartment. As I got out and climbed the stairs, I could hear our phone ringing. I hurried upstairs to answer it. It was my sister, Jessica's mother.

"Hi, Andy," she said.

I knew exactly what she was going to say before she said anything else.

"We'll take her," I said. But my unexpected answer did not register with her.

"Andy, we have been trying to get in touch with you all afternoon. Frank and I have spent the day at our attorney's office drawing up our wills and making legal arrangements for Jessica if something happened to—"

"We'll take Jessica ourselves," I interrupted.

"That's what I wanted to ask you! We need to let our attorney know that you would be willing to adopt Jessica if we were not around."

"I know," I said. "It's already been decided!"

Then there was a silence as Beth and I did a mental double take as we realized that the love of a precious little child had just connected us across time and space.

When I was in the middle of my unrecognized stroke, my other sister, April, startled me with a text. We don't speak with her very often, and texting is not our usual means of communication. In fact, she had never sent me a text, ever. Yet, at 11:27 a.m. in the middle of her busy work day, she suddenly dropped everything she was doing, reached for her cell phone, and carefully typed the following two messages:

I'm wondering how you're doing. I just want to catch up with you. Call me later.

Then, within seconds,

I love you!

To say that I was emotionally touched would be an understatement. Why would she express her heart to me on this ordinary morning? She had never done anything like this before. *Does she know that I am in trouble and could die?* I thought.

I looked at the message over and over with a lump in my throat as I felt her unconditional love for me. "I love you, too," I said to myself.

April's message made me realize how important my life was to my family. With her wakeup call, I opened the kitchen drawer and took out a pencil and notecard and wrote out my medical history, just in case I might not be conscious by the time I arrived in the emergency department. When I finished, still not thinking completely clearly, I made my way to the door to walk outside, but before I got to the door, I handed my wife, Cynthia, the notecard and said, "Get me to the hospital."

Cynthia could tell from my demeanor that this was urgent. We made our way to the car and rushed to the emergency department. There I went right up to the reception desk and announced that I was having a stroke. My pronouncement set into motion a protocol that included emergency brain scans, blood tests, and the administration of medication to help thin my blood to prevent stroke progression. When there was a lull in the action, I reached for my phone and with fingers that I could finally coordinate, typed the following response to April:

I love you too.
I'll talk to you later.

By the next morning, I was feeling much better, and most of the numbness had left my leg and face. As I was contemplating the events of the prior day, my sister April called.

"I've been very concerned about you. Cynthia called to let me know what happened."

"What made you text me minutes after my stroke started yesterday morning?" I asked. "You never sent me a text before."

"I couldn't help myself," she said. "I was overcome with an impression that I needed to text you with a message immediately, and I knew I needed to say something important. The only thing that came to my mind was, 'I love you.'"

"That message brought me back to the reality of the situation and made me realize I was having a stroke. It probably prevented me from being permanently paralyzed. Thanks for saving me with your heart," I said.

That experience happened three years ago, but our family has continued to be connected in ways that I cannot fully explain, transcending even life and death. I know that the common denominator is *love*. Love overcomes all. Love is the universal force. God is love (1 John 4:8).

PART FOUR
PRAYER

~

CHAPTER 22

PRAYING FOR A MIRACLE

~

THOMAS MARSHALL, MD

AS BARB BECAME PROGRESSIVELY MORE disabled by her multiple sclerosis, she elected to enroll in hospice. To qualify for this compassionate home nursing program, her life expectancy needed to be less than six months. I don't think this was an exaggeration, since Barb was confined to bed, her body contracted in a permanent fetal position, with a tracheostomy tube in her neck to provide oxygen to her compromised lungs, and a feeding tube in her stomach, since she could no longer swallow. Her hands were so permanently flexed that her fingers nearly touched her wrists.

I had known Barb for over ten years, but just recently assumed her care from a colleague who was moving out of the area. It was hard for me to see her so debilitated. She couldn't leave her room, so I made periodic house calls, but there was really nothing I could do at this point. Her parents were incredibly supportive, as were the members of her church. Pastor Bailie, her minister, agreed with my dismal prognosis and, when he saw her the week before, told me that he thought it would be the last time he would see her alive.

Barbara's illness started when she was in high school, at age fifteen. At the time, she was a gymnast, played the flute in the orchestra, and was active in a church youth group. She remembers not being able to grasp the rings in gym, and then slipping and falling down. At first her family thought she was clumsy. She occasionally tripped or bumped into a wall while walking, and her classmates, thinking that she had been drinking, whispered about her behind her back, and sadly, even began to shun her.

When Barbara first consulted her doctor, she was referred to a local neurologist. He ordered multiple tests and scans, but no cause could be found. This was in the late 1960s when we did not have CT scanners, MRIs, and all the sophisticated imaging and diagnostics we have today. She was sent to medical centers with the same baffling conclusions. Multiple sclerosis was considered, but she seemed too young for that. All the while she continued to deteriorate. Her handwriting was the next function she lost. She became embarrassed to write in front of others because of her trembling hands, and her writing looked like it came from the hand of a ninety-year-old. She went through a period of questioning her worth and feeling helpless.

With supreme effort, Barbara graduated from high school. However, when she enrolled in college, she developed double vision and had to drop out because she could not physically keep up. She was devastated. Before her illness, she was involved with multiple school activities, and now she could not even keep up with her basic courses. It was 1970, and, by this time, her symptoms and her diagnostic tests, including spinal taps, confirmed the diagnosis of progressive multiple sclerosis. The prognosis was not good, but she was determined to do the best she could in everything she did.

At times, the disease seemed to become inactive, a common occurrence in multiple sclerosis, with relapses and remissions, but she never improved. She would get through a crisis, and then stabilize on a plateau that was lower than her last remission. In the early 1970s, she had two respiratory arrests because the muscles of breathing were affected, requiring emergency hospitalization.

During her remissions, she was able to return to college as a handicapped student and work as a secretary. But her efforts to be "normal" were always interrupted by the progression of her disease. She could not clear her secretions, and, with a paralyzed diaphragm, was recurrently hospitalized for pneumonias and asthma. Then came one of the most humiliating problems for a young woman: losing the ability to control urination and bowels. She had to have a catheter permanently placed into her bladder and an ileostomy created in her abdomen, with a bag attached for her bowels.

Her breathing became progressively more difficult, and she was referred to the Mayo Clinic in 1978 for a second opinion. She now needed continuous oxygen, and her muscles and joints were becoming contracted and deformed because she could not move or exercise them. Mayo was her last hope, but they had no recommendations to help stop this progressive wasting disease except to pray for a miracle.

When her MS was first diagnosed, Barbara admitted to losing faith in a supreme being. Why would God allow such a devastating disease to ravish an innocent young girl? But as she matured, and with the love and counseling of her minister,

Pastor Bailie, she grew stronger in her belief that a loving God participates in our lives. Everyone in her church and community was praying for her.

Despite all the efforts, her condition continued to deteriorate, and she began to lose her vision and soon could not read anymore. She became legally blind and could hardly move out of her bed. A lung collapsed and required a large tube to be placed in her chest to expand the lung. Then in 1980, to add to her humiliation, she required the creation of a tracheostomy, a hole in her neck for a breathing tube connected to oxygen to keep her from being chronically short of breath.

At this point, I sat down with Barb and her family and explained that it was just a matter of time before she would die, since the next major infection would likely take her. We all agreed not to do any heroics, including no CPR and no further hospitalization. This would only prolong the inevitable. Our meeting ended in a tearful prayer.

June 7, 1981, a Sunday, was her sister Jan's birthday. Barb was looking forward to the celebration at their home. She tried to help with the birthday preparations but being out of bed was too exhausting for her, even with her power wheelchair equipped with oxygen to her tracheostomy tube. Her first visitor was her Aunt Ruthie, who read cards and letters written to Barb after her tragic story aired on a local radio station, WMBI. Their program asked for prayers and letters for people who were terminally ill. There were so many letters that Aunt Ruthie had trouble carrying the large mail bag. Almost every letter included a prayer for Barb to be healed. The response was overwhelming.

In the early afternoon, two girlfriends came to visit after church. Barb became weary with all the attention and was quiet while the girls made small talk. When there was a lull in the conversation, a man's voice spoke from behind Barb—but there was no man in the room! The words were clear and articulate and spoken with great authority, but also with great compassion. The voice said, "My child, get up and walk!"

Barb turned around. No one was standing there, but she knew immediately who was speaking. "I don't know what you are going to think about this," she announced, "but God just told me to get up and walk."

Her friends suddenly became very quiet.

"I know he really did," Barb insisted. "Run and get my family. I want them here with us!"

Her friends, recognizing the urgency in Barb's voice, bounded to the doorway to yell for her family, "Come quick; come quick!"

Barb felt compelled to do immediately what she was divinely instructed, so she literally jumped out of bed and removed her oxygen. She was standing on legs that had not supported her for years. Her vision was back, and she was no longer short of breath, even without her oxygen. Her contractions were gone, and she could move her feet and hands freely.

As she walked out of the room, she was first met by her mother who immediately dropped to her knees and felt Barb's calves. "You have muscles again!" she yelled. Her father came running in next, hugged Barb, and whisked her off for a waltz around the family room. A distressed occupational therapist tried to restart her oxygen, but after she realized what was happening, she simply said, "This contradicts everything I ever learned in school."

At the request of Barb's mother, everyone moved into the living room to offer a prayer. Barb sat down on the couch but was so excited that she could sit and get up that she went up and down at least ten times before she could sit still for the tearful prayer of thanksgiving offered by her mother.

That evening, Pastor Bailie was leading the worship service at Wheaton Wesleyan Church. Barb was anxious to reveal the miracle to all of her church friends, but she was late. She had no clothes to wear. All of her regular dresses had been given away years ago when she became contracted and essentially bedridden. Finally a neighbor was able to bring over a dress and some shoes, and they headed off to church. As they arrived at the building, Barb bounded up the front stairs ahead of her parents. She waited in the back of the church until Pastor Bailie asked if there were any announcements from the congregation. Barbara then stepped into the center aisle, and, as she casually strolled toward the front, she could feel her heart pounding.

Pastor Bailie, the first to see her, fell against the pulpit and began to murmur over and over, "This is nice, this is very nice, this is nice..."

When members of the congregation looked back a sudden cacophony of whispers came from all parts of the church.

"Who is that?" came from the front.

"That's Barb!" came from the back.

"There's Barb!"

"Look, there's Barb Cummiskey!"

"I thought she was sick!"

"Look at Barb Cummiskey walking down the aisle! She's *walking!*"

"*That's Barb Cummiskey!*"

Everyone started clapping, and then, as if led by a divine conductor, the entire congregation began to sing.

Amazing grace, how sweet the sound
That saved a wretch like me
I once was lost but now I'm found
Was blind but now I see...

Tears of joy ran down every face. Pastor Bailie eventually regained his composure and invited Barb to come to the front to tell her amazing story. There was no sermon, but that was a service no one will ever forget.

The next day was a Monday, and Barb called our office for an appointment. My nurse didn't know what to say when she called. But the greatest surprise was when I saw her in the hallway of our office, walking toward me. I thought I was seeing an apparition! Here was my patient, who was not expected to live another week, totally cured. I stopped all of her medication and took out her bladder catheter, but she wasn't quite ready to have the tracheostomy tube removed until another visit. No one had ever seen anything like this before. That afternoon, we sent Barb for a chest X-ray. Her lungs were now perfectly normal, with the collapsed lung totally expanded with no infiltrate or other abnormality that had existed before.

I have never witnessed anything like this before or since and considered it a rare privilege to observe the Hand of God performing a true miracle. Barb has gone on to live a normal life in every way. She subsequently married a minister and feels her calling in life is to serve others, which is what she did after her life was miraculously preserved by her Creator.

CHAPTER 23

THREE-WAY PHONE CALL TO HEAVEN

~◡

SCOTT J. KOLBABA, MD

IT WAS A ROUTINE ADMISSION for asthma. My partner had seen Sharon in the emergency department the day before, and she was wheezing. Recovering from knee surgery, she was living temporarily with her daughter who smoked and had cats and dogs, all of which irritated her lungs. So it was not unexpected, four months after her surgery, that she would have an asthma attack. My partner, Dr. John Born, warned her to stay out of that environment and return home. This is what she had planned to do, but it was now too late.

"Murphy's Law" applies to medical practice, just like it does in everyday life. A crisis always seems to happen on a Friday afternoon when you are ready to go away for the weekend. This is exactly when Sharon showed up in the emergency department. Dr. Born stopped by the hospital on his way home to see if Sharon was well enough to be discharged. Under those circumstances, it is very tempting to send her home for office follow-up. This is what the emergency department physician was recommending, but Dr. Born had a strange feeling that she needed to be in the hospital. He admitted her and called me to follow over the weekend in his absence.

The next day, I saw her for the first time. I could hear the wheezes in her lungs, but she thought she was doing better. I made the necessary adjustments in her medications, reducing her cortisone, which is used routinely for a bad asthma attack. Her chest X-ray showed what looked like an early pneumonia, so I added an antibiotic to cover all of the organisms she could have picked up.

The next morning on rounds, the nurses reported that she had gotten a little worse, and I was mentally scolding myself for too quickly reducing her cortisone dose the day before. When I walked into the room, she was on the phone. Normally, when I make rounds, patients tell their callers that the doctor just came in, and they needed to hang up. I always thought this was a little pompous on my part to expect some-one to hang up the phone because they were preempted by the doctor, but it was certainly nice, and it made rounds quicker.

This day, Sharon did not hang up the phone, so I pulled up a chair and sat patiently. It was a little awkward when she closed her eyes to listen on the phone. It seemed like a silent eternity. I did not know where to put my hands or if I should look up or down. My mind wandered as I shifted my body in the chair. I thought about her illness and whether I should be concerned about her slow progress. *Am I missing something?* I dismissed the thought. Then it came back again. *Should I order any additional tests?* No. But something kept arguing with what I thought was my logical scientific reasoning, and I finally gave in and decided to order a D-dimer blood test.

I am not sure why I was drawn to this lab, but it is a test that helps diagnose pulmonary emboli (blood clots in the lung). It seemed a little overkill to me at the time to be looking for a third diagnosis when we had two satisfactory reasons for her asthma attack: her daughter's animals and the pneumonia. But I wrote the order to relieve my mental conflict and went on to my next patient.

The lab was prompt in running it. Normal is three hundred or less, but her level was eighteen hundred, one of the highest I had ever seen. I immediately ordered a CT scan of her lungs. Two hours later, I was interrupted with a call from the radiologist. Sharon had showers of life-threatening blood clots in her lungs, and later we found clots in both legs.

My next call was to Sharon. "I'm sorry to let you know that you have blood clots throughout both lungs. You will need to move to the step-down unit for closer monitoring and be started on blood thinners."

"It was the prayer," she said.

"What prayer?" I asked.

"When you made rounds and were waiting for me, my lay minister was on the phone and said a prayer that my doctor would be guided to the correct diagnosis. That's why you ordered that test."

I wondered if it was just a coincidence that I happened to think about ruling out blood clots at the same time that she was praying for help. But Sharon knew the answer. To her, it was nothing short of a miracle. After her Internet research, she knew that if blood clots were not diagnosed early, they could be fatal. She was convinced that I had simply been spliced into her three-way call with heaven.

Sharon did well after the diagnosis was made and left the hospital four days later, feeling much better.

I felt better too, after getting some much-needed help from heaven.

CHAPTER 24

JASON THE JET

~

JOHN M. SARAN, MD

IT HAD BEEN A VERY busy few months in my internal medicine practice, and I recognized that I was suffering from burnout. I needed a vacation. My wife, Janet, and I could only take a few days, so we decided on an extended weekend retreat far away from our home in Chicago. We picked the date, and then studied a map of the United States. A trip to upper New York State with a drive into Canada sounded perfect. With visions of being all alone, we made reservations on Southwest Airlines and arranged for a rental car.

A month before the trip, I had a strange feeling that New York was not where we should be going, so I impulsively called the airline and canceled our trip. That night, we opened the map again. Some of our friends enjoyed San Antonio, Texas, and it sounded interesting, so I called Southwest and booked our trip. But, again, after a few days, I had the same unusual feeling, so I canceled the San Antonio flight and hotel as well. Texas was not where we needed to go.

Back to the drawing board. As we studied the map, we were both drawn to Salt Lake City, Utah. We could stay in a secluded part of Robert Redford's Sundance Ski Resort, where we could close the door and not see anyone for three days. I called Southwest again, but they were unable to accommodate both of us on one plane. My wife, Janet, would have a separate flight with a layover in Denver. It seemed a little strange to be so enthusiastic about a weekend trip with Janet and not fly with her, but I booked the flights and the room at Sundance. This felt right. The day before we left, a cancellation on my flight allowed Janet to fly with me after all. I brought some books and planned on sleeping, eating, and reading, in that order.

I'm usually compulsive about getting boarding passes early, but, for some reason, we both forgot and ended up boarding at the end of the C line, the final group. When we got on the plane, the only seats were the last two on the right, just in front of the galley.

It was so early in the morning that I didn't pay attention to anything except getting to my seat and parking myself for a morning nap. The flight attendant came to discuss something with the young woman in front of me, and I was going to ask if I could help, but I was too tired to do anything and promptly fell asleep. Janet stayed awake and watched as the flight attendants kept going back and forth, trying to help with the young lady, who appeared to be in pain. She thought about waking me up, but then decided that I really needed my rest.

An hour later, I was suddenly awakened by an anxious captain on the PA system.

"Excuse me, this is the captain speaking. We have a medical emergency on the plane; a passenger is delivering a baby. Is there a doctor on the flight? If so, please raise your hand so the flight crew can see where you are."

Now I was wide awake. I put my arm up, but when I discovered that there were no other doctors on the flight, I broke into a cold sweat. I had not delivered a baby since medical school thirty years before. I hoped the baby could wait until we made an emergency landing in Denver.

Three members of the flight crew hurried to my side. We made brief introductions.

"Dr. Saran, Emily [the girl in front of me] is in labor! Could you deliver the baby in the galley?"

We helped Emily back to the galley and pulled the curtain. There were three flight attendants, a psychiatric nurse, a school nurse, Emily, and myself, all crowded into the tiny space. Emily was lying down now and I did a brief examination. What I found gave me even more anxiety. The due date for the baby was a month away, but this baby wasn't going to wait till we landed in Denver; the baby's head was visible and crowning! I would have to deliver a baby within the next few minutes. I closed my eyes, bowed my head, and said silently, "God, please have angels guide my hands. Amen."

When I opened my eyes, Emily was pushing, and the baby was coming out.

"I need a blanket," I said to one of the flight attendants. Unfortunately, the airline no longer carried blankets, but one of the passengers heard my voice and handed the nervous flight attendant her child's personal blanket.

Emily was now delivering. I took a deep breath. *I know I can do this*, I said to myself. *I am the most qualified on this plane. I have to do it!*

With one more push, the baby was out. Small but healthy looking, he cried immediately and urinated on one of the nurses. I knew these were both good signs and was relieved. I had a pair of emergency rubber gloves on, but I had blood all over my shirt, pants, glasses, and hair. The captain came on the PA system and announced that the plane had departed with 150 passengers but now had 151, but the new passenger had no luggage. Everyone on the plane spontaneously applauded, and I couldn't help but smile.

We wrapped the baby in the borrowed blanket. Now I had to find something to cut the umbilical cord and tie it off. We had no scissors except for some passenger's blunt-end child's type scissors. I reached for my shoes, removed the laces, and tied one onto the umbilical cord. I also used a string from a nurse's hooded sweatshirt and cut in between with the tiny scissors. (Alan Edmonds Shoes even sent me a new pair of shoes after the story broke since I used their laces to help with the birth.)

When we landed in Denver, they took Emily and her new baby off the plane and into a waiting ambulance. During the brief layover, I hurried into the terminal and found a shower in the employee section and cleaned up. I returned to the plane without much fanfare, but when I arrived in Salt Lake City, I was met by an army of reporters and photographers. I was happy to get to the quiet of the mountains, but when we pulled into the lodge, there were satellite trucks parked in front with reporters ready for my interview.

Good Morning America was now on the phone after they called my son and father to locate me. I needed to wake up at 4 a.m. for a 7 a.m. (EST) live broadcast. The weekend continued with unabated phone calls and reporters knocking on the door of my "secluded" retreat. My quiet interlude away from everyone turned into an interview with the world.

By Monday morning, I was anxious to get to the airport and back to the peace of my practice. We boarded the Southwest plane and made our way to our seats. As I walked down the aisle, I recognized many faces returning to Chicago, and many whispered, "There's the doctor who delivered the baby." I was asked to autograph a number of boarding passes as we made our way to the only remaining seats on the plane, the exact seats we occupied a few days before. I enjoyed being a celebrity for a day.

We arrived late into Chicago, but I was thankful to be home. On the way, I thought about my experience and realized that our prior reservations were canceled for a reason. My quiet vacation was not to be. Instead, God had a different plan for me, and I was humbled to find I had been chosen to be His servant.

Almost one year later I received a touching thank you letter from the baby's adoptive parents, but the most moving part of the correspondence was the photograph; a picture of a proud young child, chest out, dressed in a bomber flight jacket with the nametag that read, "Jason the Jet."

CHAPTER 25

THE MORNING MIRACLE

~

DAVID GIESER, MD

Western Union Telegram
September 17, 1966
To: Kenneth Gieser
Lausanne, Switzerland
From: Kay Gieser
Wheaton, Illinois, USA
David injured **Stop** *May lose kidney* **Stop** *Come home immediately*
Stop

I can only imagine what my father thought when he received this telegram about me. He had taken a business trip to Lausanne, Switzerland, when I was in high school. Transatlantic phone lines were not well developed at that time, and the only way we could reliably communicate was by Western Union telegram.

The story that led to this telegram began in the fall of my senior year in high school during gym class. We had been playing soccer during the last several sessions, and although this was only gym class, the games were competitive. I enjoyed being goalie, and, as I approached my position for today's game, I didn't realize that this particular scrimmage would bring both extreme suffering as well as extreme growth.

It was a warm fall day with a hint of burning leaves in the air. I took off my sweatshirt, and, as I loosened up, I resolved to block any shot that came anywhere near me. My below-average performance from the previous game was still in the back of my mind. As the game started, I was keyed up and ready. One shot blocked and then another. I was getting into a rhythm.

Toward the end of the game, our opponents were success-fully changing the momentum. The pressure was on. The midfielder advanced on my right and passed the ball to an advancing forward on my left. I charged him to cut down his angle to the net. As he kicked, I dove for the ball. The for-ward, however, couldn't stop his kicking motion, and struck me directly in my left flank. It was the most excruciating pain I have ever experienced.

As I lay on the ground, I think I passed out for a few sec-onds. I tried to pretend that I was not badly hurt, but I could not restrain the agony on my face and the tears in my eyes. To this day, I don't how I did it, but I slowly got to my knees, stood, and then punted the ball downfield. Moments later, the game was over. I hobbled off the field and collapsed onto the bench.

I knew this was serious. I was wounded in a way I had never experienced before. Very slowly, leaning to the left as I walked, I went to the gym, showered, dressed, and headed to my last class. The bus ride home was sheer agony. I stumbled out the bus door, literally groaning with each step. As I strug-gled home, I periodically leaned against a tree to rest.

When I finally made it to my front door, I shuffled down the hall and slid onto my bed, totally exhausted. My mother heard the commotion and ran to see what had happened. One look at me and she knew that I needed immediate medical attention. I leaned on her shoulder as we made our way to the car and drove directly to my doctor's office. One of the advantages of being mortally wounded was that I did not have to wait to be seen. Dr. Wyngarden saw me immediately and recognized the severity of my problem. He picked up the phone and called the ambulance to take me to our local thirty-five-bed hospital.

The ambulance was a vintage converted Cadillac with a white top and a maroon body. Every bump in the road caused excruciating pain in my flank. But the true highlight of the ride was when the ambulance overheated on the way to the hospital and had to stop at a service station to fill the radiator with water! It was not funny at the time, but it makes me laugh now to think about that scene with an old Cadillac, siren blaring, single light flashing, pulling into the service station to pop the hood and fill the radiator.

When I got to the hospital, I took Demerol, a narcotic pain medication. Although it caused some nausea and sleepiness, it gave me temporary relief from the searing pain in my side.

When I think back to those next days, it was a blur. I remember the severe pain and the frightening red color of my urine. I was confined to bed rest, and the highlight of my day was seeing my doctor with his gray flat-top haircut. He rounded twice a day, and, each time, he carefully concealed his concern about my injury. I am thankful I didn't know that he was anticipating the need to remove my ruptured kidney.

I also didn't know that he asked my mother to telegram my father so he could be there for my operation.

My injury happened on a Tuesday. It was now Friday. I was convinced I would never get better, and I knew that everyone else thought that too. I watched the clock on the wall with tears in my eyes that blurred the numbers. Eight, nine, ten o'clock.

Then something happened that was sudden and totally unexpected. My pain vanished. It was not something gradual, like you would normally expect with an injury. One minute I was enduring the pain, and the next, I was totally pain free. At first I was hesitant to move at all, expecting the pain would return like a dagger in my side. I lay very still for a very long time, simply enjoying my respite. But then I had to see if it was really gone.

First, I slowly turned to the right. I waited, but nothing happened. Then I inched cautiously to the left. So far, so good. But the ultimate test would be to sit up in bed. It took more than a few minutes to muster enough courage to attempt. I moved the back of the bed up and then, ever so gradually, pulled myself to a sitting position. I had no pain at all. When my doctor made afternoon rounds, he could not believe I could be healed so suddenly, so he kept me in the hospital two additional days believing my severe pain would return at any time. But it did not. I was totally pain free.

My father arrived from Europe the next day and brought with him a new portable tape recorder that he purchased in Holland. It was not available in this country yet, and I was thrilled. I spent the next week in the infirmary of the local college, and then finally went home for additional recovery.

All told, I was out of school for six weeks, but my pain never returned after that remarkable Friday morning.

I was excited to get back to school. All of my friends and classmates gave me warm smiles and greetings. I never realized how much concern there had been for my well-being.

I will never forget the conversation I had with a favorite teacher. "David," he said, "we were very concerned about you. Every day, someone came up to me to ask about you. And then, when we heard that you might lose your kidney, a group of faculty members gathered together for a special prayer for you right before chapel at ten o'clock on that Friday after you were injured."

When I heard the time, I was suddenly overwhelmed with emotion. A tear welled up in my eye. Now I knew. The faithful prayers of the faculty were answered with a miracle.

Approximately eight months later, I was seen at the Mayo Clinic in Rochester, Minnesota, for an unrelated problem. As a part of my evaluation, a specialized X-ray of my kidney, known as an intravenous pyelogram, was performed. A urologist spent several minutes studying the films. Finally, he looked over at me and said, "I see no sign of the injury. Your kidney is normal."

CHAPTER 26

FASTING FOR A FAMILY

~〜

JOHN SHOWALTER, MD

OUR DAUGHTER, BECKY, HAD ALWAYS wanted a large family. As a teenager, she once declared that she wanted twelve children! Though we suspected that her enthusiasm would fade over time, we would never have anticipated the devastation that a diagnosis of infertility would bring.

Becky and Eric were married during their final year of college, in December 1990. It was the most wonderful celebration and party that I had ever attended (or paid for, for that matter), and this young couple was a match made in heaven. Both were ardently committed to their faith and to each other, and, to make things even better, their temperaments, personalities, and talents were perfectly complementary. The world was exactly as it "should be."

Because they attended different schools and had one semester to complete, special arrangements were made for Becky to finish her education with Eric in Florida. Considering Becky's previous declarations and Eric's great love of children, we fully expected that grandchildren would be right around the corner, particularly because they also vowed to adhere to the principle of natural family planning, which we all know is stronger on the "family" component than it is on the "planning."

A year went by, and we thought they were particularly skilled in the family planning method because of the need to balance the cost of graduate school with the reality of limited income. Then another year passed, and yet another. Finally, in 1993, they told us they had been seeing a fertility specialist in Ohio who was not optimistic about their chances of having a family at all. No matter what interventions they undertook, nothing "worked," yet they remained steadfast in their commitment to avoid unnatural methods of conception such as in vitro fertilization, because of the inevitable destruction of human life. To add to the grief of the diagnosis, the insensitive specialist also suggested that they try at all costs to avoid pregnancy "because the fetus would probably have congenital defects anyway."

We received the news with incredible sadness for Becky and Eric, because we knew how much they wanted to have a family. Uninformed as I was, and to some degree because I refused to believe the results of their tests, I made the honest, but hurtful, suggestion that stress was probably the culprit. That was just another lesson in the concept: "Open mouth... insert foot." But my embarrassment at my faux pas was not nearly as painful as the realization that our daughter's dream of her own children would never come to pass.

At that point I made the commitment to do whatever I could to help. But what *could* I do? Helplessness is not a good hand to deal to a physician, especially an orthopedic surgeon. After all, we are trained to *fix* things!

It was the spring of 1993, and with no material way to help, I decided that I would commit to fast from everything except water every Thursday. In my Catholic faith we believe that fasting and prayer are the best ways to request help from God. And so it started. Each Thursday, as the hunger pangs grew, I began to pray for Becky and Eric. Reminders to pray came at any time, especially increasing as each hour passed, but I was determined to do this until I received an answer.

Meanwhile, Becky and Eric were diligently pursuing international adoption through an agency that would attempt to match them with an infant in Mexico. The process was arduous, complicated, expensive, and frustrating, but they maintained good spirits throughout. Months passed with no results from the agency and, unfortunately, none from my fasting and prayer either. 1993 became 1994, and still no results from Mexico.

I had been fasting for over a year and was becoming fatigued in the process, wondering why I was even bothering to continue. Some progress had been made in Mexico, but each step forward seemed to be met with at least a half step back. Finally, in the second week of June, I decided that I had had enough. I felt extremely guilty for giving up, but I just couldn't go on. Besides, the adoption process appeared to be progressing to a positive conclusion, so there would indeed be a baby in the family.

Becky and Eric kept us informed of the adoption process, so we were not surprised when they called in late July to say that everything was in motion for a baby to arrive in March of 1995, but...it would *not be from Mexico*. Becky was pregnant! They explained that they wanted to be absolutely certain before calling, and told us that this would be a tenuous pregnancy, certainly high risk, but they had their baby!

It was then that I confided that I had given up on my program of fasting and praying, and they asked when that occurred. I remembered the exact week because my guilt would not let me forget that I had quit. What is most remarkable is that when I gave them the date, they exclaimed in incredible amazement that it was the same week that they had attended a retreat and Jacob, our first grandson, had been conceived. Only then did I realize that I had not grown tired and quit, but that God had spoken silently that my work was over; fasting and praying for this infertility was no longer needed. What I thought was a source of guilt and failure was, in reality, God saying that he had heard!

Our prayer was not over, however, because the pregnancy was indeed high risk. Many physician visits, ultrasounds, and a myriad of tests were needed, especially since an excessive accumulation of amniotic fluid portended danger. Yet, Becky made it to full term, and, on March 11, 1995, our first grandson, and our first miracle, Jacob, was born...perfect in every way!

But the story doesn't end there. Becky's dream and prayer for a large family would be heard and honored abundantly. She hasn't reached twelve, but they have come pretty darned close!

On May 18, 1997, bouncing Ben (Ben-Ben) was born, now a young man with endless energy and amazing artistic talent.

On January 26, 1999, Rachel (Pippi) arrived and has become a beautiful and poised young lady who, paradoxically, is probably the toughest of all the children.

On January 17, 2000, Emmanuel (Manny) arrived from Haiti, just after his first birthday. The adoption from Mexico never came through, but Becky and Eric continued to have a heart for adoption, and Emmanuel was born one month before Rachel.

Providential involvement with a charity that promoted education for the poorest of the poor in Haiti led Becky and Eric to find a happy baby with huge bright eyes and an ear-to-ear grin that captured their hearts. At the time, he was in the Hospital for Dying Children in Haiti. The adoption was finalized within months, and Manny became part of the family before his first birthday. Now Manny (variously Dooper, Super-Dooper or "The Haitian Sensation") is a robust, athletic schmoozer and also the family mystic with spiritual insights that marvel even adults.

On November 11, 2001, Elijah (Moe) arrived and is now an energetic adolescent with an intellect to rival any thirteen-year-old (grandparental pride aside).

On February 17, 2005, Judah (Bear) arrived and has a heart as big as they come and a gift for gentle forgiveness that is exceptional for his age. His goal in life is to become a priest.

On September 7, 2007, Danny (Bananny or Little Man) arrived and is now a young boy with intellect and humor that keeps the family laughing.

On February 24, 2010, Genevieve (Evie) arrived and, as you might expect being the youngest of eight, is the most precocious in every way, smart, challenging, and as charming as a young lady can be.

And what about the first miracle, Jacob, you ask? He is now nineteen years old and is an accomplished vocalist and actor who is a college sophomore, studying musical theater with one of the country's premier operatic performers.

Fasting and praying for my daughter was a truly humbling experience for me, filled with important life lessons. I learned the value of patience, a trait that has not been one of my strong suits. As a surgeon, I am able to fix nearly every orthopedic problem quickly, in surgery. In this case, I agonized for well over a year before prayers were answered. Second, I discovered that the love that exists between family members is one of the strongest forces in the universe. I believe that my fasting and prayer contributed at least in a small way to the miracle of life in our family. Finally, I learned the joy of answered prayer. When I felt totally helpless, I turned to fasting and prayer, and my prayer was indeed answered, and much more abundantly than I would have ever dreamed.

Conclusion: What Doctors Taught Me

~

Scott J. Kolbaba, MD

I DON'T GOLF.

I know that sounds like heresy, a doctor who doesn't golf! Can I really be a doctor?

I have played golf before, probably as many as ten times in my life. I even have a set of golf clubs, but, over the years, my sons Dane and Nate and probably Ian, whom we fondly refer to as our "perfect son," have used them to hit rocks, and now they are full of nicks. However, the way I play, I'm sure the dents would hardly detract from my game. I actually enjoy golf, but with seven children and an unpredictable job, I find it difficult to get away for any length of time. In addition, every time I hit a divot, which my golfing friends tell me is launching a clump of sod instead of the ball, I hurt my back or neck. And I seem to be the divot expert.

What do I do in my spare time, you ask. Well, as a primary care internist, I am up at five every morning to make hospital rounds before office hours at eight. I get home at six if no one is admitted to the hospital, and then often have some catch up to do in addition to helping with children's homework. I have gone through eighth grade eight times. I do like growing pumpkins, and we have been the champion pumpkin growers in the Sycamore Pumpkin Contest (one of the largest festivals in Illinois) two years running. I love to walk my dog, but since she is a giant Newfoundland, she is usually the one taking me for the walk to get my exercise. My real joy, however, is vacationing with family, and everyone seems to be able to make it year after year. We are now up to twenty-five vacationers, newborn to sixty-seven years old.

What's the point of all this?

I think people are surprised when they find out what makes physicians tick, what they like to do, and why they became doctors. Most of my physician friends don't talk, even to their colleagues, about their true feelings on life, career, family, and spirituality. In my interviews with over two hundred physicians, I believe the majority shared their heartfelt feelings, which surprised me. I think one reason is that I am close friends with many of these doctors, and there is a comfort in that and in knowing many others shared their feelings too. But the real reason, I believe, is a sincere desire to share with the world their passion for family, their regard for hard work and determination, and their knowledge that there is a higher power. Their revelations were so touching that I had to share some of the best in this chapter.

DOCTORS "SAVE THE WORLD"

Some time ago I learned about Emily, a young girl from Romania, who was available for adoption, but who would probably never be placed because of badly deformed feet that prevented her from walking. When our family visited Romania as part of an adoption advocacy mission, we went to some of the orphanages similar to where Emily was living and came away wanting to adopt everyone. The smell of urine from the state orphanage was evident one block away, and there was an eerie silence in the nursery because the babies learn that crying does not accomplish anything, so they stop crying. We entered the "dying room," which had a quiet sacredness from babies too ill to make a sound, soon to meet their Creator due to lack of medicine and medical care.

On a particularly cold night in her orphanage, Emily tried to stay warm by keeping her feet close to a space heater. After she fell asleep, her plastic shoes melted, badly burning her feet. The resulting deformities and scarring would require multiple operations by highly specialized orthopedic surgeons before she could walk. She was now relegated to crawling and would probably never walk normally. When I learned about this poor orphan, I mentioned her in casual conversation to my cardiology friend, Dr. Andrew Rauh, who loves children and has successfully raised a large family of his own. A week later, I received this surprising call from him.

"You know that little girl with the burned feet?" he said on the phone.

"Yes," I said.

"Well, I spoke with my wife, and we'll take her."

"What do you mean?" I asked, not sure of his real intent.

"We want to adopt her."

"But you don't know anything about her," I said.

"We don't need to," he said. "We can provide the medical care she will need for whatever she has, and we want her to join our family."

I was initially amazed that he would make such a commitment to adopt without even a meeting. But that apparently was not an issue for him. He recognized a young child in trouble and was willing to take Emily under his wing to give her a chance at a normal life. Unfortunately for Dr. and Mrs. Rauh, Emily's story touched another couple just days before they made their decision, and she was no longer available for adoption. What I find most revealing about this story, however, is that it illustrates the compassion of many of the doctors I interviewed. Like Dr. and Mrs. Rauh, a surprising number of the doctors I know would have made the same decision.

In fact, most of my colleagues have a similar desire to do some good in the world by helping others. It became such a recurrent theme that I began to fondly refer to this group, of which I am a card-carrying member, as the "sappy do-gooders." They recognize that becoming a physician is a privilege, and they look for opportunities to use their skills and talents to help the less fortunate.

Dr. David Gieser, ophthalmologist and authority in glaucoma, regularly travels to distant corners of the third world to teach ophthalmologists new techniques in eye surgery. One of the problems he encountered was that many physicians could not afford to travel to hear his lecture series, so he started to anonymously fund the cost of their travel and lodging.

He told me this harrowing story of one of his trips to a location that I have taken off my "bucket list" for family vacations.

"The streets of the capital city of the central African country we were visiting were empty. Our driver, taking my wife, Mary, and me back to the hotel after my dinner lecture, was driving his aging VW bus at dangerously high speeds. Just hours before, during the day, the city was a bustling marketplace. Now there were absolutely no cars on the streets, and not one person was visible, anywhere. It was an eerie sight. I asked what was happening and why he was going so fast with no one around.

"'Well, sir,' said the driver in broken English, 'we are in the midst of a civil war, and, at night, the rebels come down from the hills and shoot anything that moves.'

"Mary shifted uncomfortably in her seat, and, after regaining my composure, I replied, 'Keep the pedal to the metal!'"

Dr. Mraz, the only female emergency room physician at our suburban hospital, loves the fast pace and the adrenalin rush of dealing with life-and-death situations. She told me she wanted to be a doctor for as long as she could remember.

"Why?" I asked.

"It started when I saw how my grandfather suffered from multiple illnesses. He was a truck driver and, while driving, he suddenly went blind from undiagnosed glaucoma. He remained unhealthy after that and died from bladder cancer when I was only five years old. I always wanted to fix him. I saw what a severe toll his illness had on our family, and I wanted to make a difference in the lives of others so that they would not have to live like my grandfather."

When I asked Dr. Steve Graham, also an emergency department doctor, why he went into medicine and what he considered his major accomplishment, he related this story.

"I can honestly say that I have never written a research paper, I have never been given a major award, and I was not the first in my medical school class (but not the last either). But what I have accomplished is my 'American dream.'

"I grew up in a working class family. My father repaired conveyer belts in a factory. When I was two years old, he left on a business trip, and, while he was away, he was hit by a drunk driver and never came home to me. I was the youngest of three children that my widowed mother raised by herself. We never had very much. I remember determining that when I grew up, I would provide a better life for my family and my children.

"My third-grade teacher, a nun in our Catholic school, changed my life with a simple statement. 'Everyone is given certain gifts by God,' she said, 'and our job is to recognize those talents and use them to the fullest.' I thought about that statement for a long time. I realized that I was good in school and in science and decided to run with those talents as far as I could.

"I was the first in our family to graduate from college, Temple University. Then I went further and entered the University of Pittsburgh School of Medicine. I knew that if I worked hard, I could provide opportunities for my children that were never available to me, while at the same time serving others. And I did. This is *my* 'American dream.'"

A Deep but Private Faith

Faith and spirituality are topics most doctors do not discuss with their colleagues or their patients, and, in my thirty years of private practice, I can think of only a handful of patients who expressed a desire to discuss their god. Physicians are concerned about being criticized if they bring faith into what is supposed to be a scientific discipline. Yet in my heart-to-heart meetings, I was impressed by the deep faith expressed by most doctors.

Dr. John Showalter, one of the first hand surgeons in the Chicagoland area to successfully reattach a severed hand, never talks about his faith. I have known him for thirty years and was surprised to learn that he fasted for one full day every week for over a year for God's intervention in helping his daughter create a family. His fasting and prayers were answered more abundantly than even he expected, with eight healthy grandchildren.

Trauma orthopedic surgeon, Steve Heim, MD, does not attend or belong to an organized church, but he freely admitted that his experience in being directed to a hypothermic skier buried in snow under a tree was unquestionably God directing him to that very location, not only to save the skier, but also to save himself.

And then there's the case of my partner, Dr. Born.

"That was a close one," said Dr. Born, after he hung up the phone with his consulting cardiologist, Dr. Tom Discher. We were sitting in our crowded little office, which we share with two nurses.

"What do you mean?" I asked, overhearing his conversation.

"I did a pre-op exam on Frank Morris last week and was ready to clear him for surgery when that little voice in the back of my head kept telling me that he needed a stress test, and the one thing I have learned over the years is to never ignore that little voice. It's never wrong."

"So did you do the stress test?" I asked.

"I advised it, but Frank refused. I finally had to tell him that if he didn't have a stress test, he wouldn't go to surgery for his increasingly painful hip. I think that convinced him. Tom [Dr. Discher] just finished his stress test, and he failed it badly. There was no perfusion to his anterior wall [indicating a block in the major artery of the heart]. He is taking him for a cath tomorrow."

Frank Morris went on to have a coronary bypass surgery the next week, a procedure that probably saved his life, since his coronary disease was so bad that he could have died from cardiac complications during his hip surgery.

Like Dr. Born, many of my colleagues and I have had similar experiences, and we eventually learn to listen to that little voice for some free advice from above.

DOCTORS AND THEIR FAMILIES

The other surprise I found in interviewing doctors was their list of priorities. I created a standard series of questions which I found generally worked well. This included, "What would you consider to be your major accomplishment in life?" It is a fairly broad question, by design, and I expected to have a wonderfully colorful series of answers like graduating from medical school, saving lives, the award for "Top Doctor," climbing a mountain, and so on. However, the answer from nearly every doctor, without hesitation, was family. They considered their families the most important part of their lives and their greatest accomplishments. I was truly surprised.

I asked the question of my good friend and orthopedic surgeon, Dr. David Mochel, and expected a story about his distinguished orthopedic career. Instead, without hesitation, he replied, "The experience of coaching my sons in their seventh and eighth grade church basketball teams."

He was the head coach, and both sons played on the team. Under his leadership, they won four consecutive championships.

"How did you do that?" I asked.

"Well, it was not so much the championships that I loved, although that was sweet. What was important to me was to spend quality time with my sons and the ability to take awkward eighth graders and give them pride and confidence in their abilities. What I learned was that each player had a talent. Some were good shooters, some could dribble well, some were defenders. I found that if I could put the players where their talent was maximized, we could not only win games, but the players realized they could positively contribute to the team. Their newfound confidence then spilled over into their studies and everything they did.

"I'll never forget Johnathan, who could not dribble or shoot, but he was a tiger on defense. If we played a standard defense and put him on the key shooter for the other team, we could totally shut the team down. And as the season progressed, our players, and then the players on the opposing teams, recognized that Johnathan, who was always picked last for everything, was now a key to our success. By the end of the season, he had earned the boys' respect and was a changed person.

"We had another young man who could do nothing well, but he had a sixth sense of where the ball was going. We practiced that talent at every scrimmage throughout the season. He would line up where he could steal the ball and run down the court and shoot a layup. Despite endless practices, he had never been successful in a real game. We were now at the end of the season in a hard-fought playoff game. We were losing by a narrow margin, and the other team had the ball. As they brought it down the court, my eyes caught Andrew's, and I nodded my head. His face became serious and determined. He moved into the position we practiced over and over and over. He stood there and waited. Everything seemed to move in slow motion. He broke! I held my breath. The ball was passed, and suddenly, out of nowhere, an athlete was sprinting down the court, all alone on his own center stage, to execute a perfect layup. It was Andrew!

"The stadium went wild. Every member of our team ran onto the court to hit the clenched hand of a player who had just made his first and most spectacular basket of the entire season. That play and the expression on Andrew's face are things I will remember the rest of my life, and more importantly, so will Andrew. His steal changed the momentum of the game, which we ultimately won.

"I was able to draw closer to my sons coaching their team, and I think they learned that basketball is a microcosm of life, where each of us has the opportunity to influence the life of someone else for the good, and, in so doing, we are better ourselves. Helping all those impressionable boys recognize that they each have God-given talents, and maximizing those talents, was life changing for all of us."

I have worked closely with Dr. Mochel for twenty years and never heard this story of love and dedication, but it illustrates what I heard over and over from the majority of doctors, all choosing to put family first.

HARD WORK AND DEDICATION
"At mile twenty-four, I went blind, and I knew that was not a good sign!"

This is what Dr. Mraz, a relatively inexperienced runner at the time, told me about her second marathon.

"I first got into running when I was working out in the gym, and my girlfriend asked me if I would like to do a marathon with her. I said, 'Sure, why not?'

"After that, I was hooked. I have done eleven marathons including three Boston Marathons, but my second was probably the most memorable. It was an unusually warm October day, and I was trying to qualify for Boston, which has strict criteria for admission. I was probably running too fast, and, at mile twenty-four, I knew it. I suddenly became dizzy, lost my vision, and threw up. I took some water, and, after sitting for a short time, I was no longer faint and my vision returned. I called my husband, who was waiting for me at the twenty-six-mile finish line, and he rushed to meet me.

"'Let's go home,' he said.

"'No, I need to finish,' I said, and finish I did, albeit with a very slow trot."

Most doctors shared their almost universal belief in hard work and commitment to accomplishing goals. I could relate to many of my colleagues who were the first in their family to even attend college. Cardiologist Dr. Patrick Fenner told me that he has never given up on anything he tried to do. This included his medical career. He was a two-sport athlete at Kalamazoo College, playing both football and basketball. Because of the time spent in athletics, his grades were not up to the usual standard for medical school admission. He went to his college advisor to discuss his intent to apply to medical school. He still remembers her exact words of "advice."

"Plenty of students come through my office, and I know the students who will make it and who won't, and you are not going to make it," she said, emphasizing her point by tapping her finger on her desk.

"I never thought she was right," he told me. "The only way I have gotten ahead in life is to not quit.

"I came from a working-class family. My father was an auto mechanic. My mother went to junior college but excelled in her career and became the supervisor of operations for admissions at Western Michigan University."

Patrick admired his mother's commitment to support the family. "She was the backbone of my family," he told me. "She worked hard and sacrificed, and I could see from her example that it paid off. I believe she taught me that in order to achieve, you have to sacrifice."

His college counselor was right about his medical school acceptance, at least initially. Patrick applied and was not accepted. He took a position at a nuclear power plant that paid more than he ever thought he could make in an entry-level job. But he still wanted to pursue medicine, so he applied again, but again received all rejection letters.

Fortunately Patrick was befriended by a concerned medical pathologist, Dr. Charles Beyerlein, who recognized his dilemma. "If you really want to get into medical school," he said, "you are going to have to go to graduate school to prove to them that you are committed to make it through medical school. You need to study for the Medical School Admissions Test and dramatically improve your scores. If you do that, you will have a good chance of getting in."

Patrick took his advice, and, without any prospect of enrolling in medical school, he resigned his power plant position and applied for graduate school at the University of Michigan. He was rejected because they thought he was too old. He was getting used to the rejection game. He then applied to Michigan State, where he was accepted as a teaching assistant. Because he had never taught before, he became so nervous he could hardly function, but he persevered and ultimately became a good teacher. At the same time, he studied the basics of chemistry, biology, math, and the other subjects on the Medical School Admissions Test (MCAT). He even took some time off to study all day and sometimes all night.

How did he do on his next MCAT?

"I killed it!" he told me with a well-earned smile. And this, combined with his A's in graduate school, convinced several medical schools to offer him a position. On his first day in medical school, he remembers looking around the class and thinking, "What am I doing here? These are all great students. Can I really do this?"

Not only did he do it, but he excelled in school, in residency in internal medicine, and in a fellowship in cardiology, his true love. His eight-year-old daughter, Peyton, summed up his struggle in one statement: "You know, Dad, if you really want to be good at something, you have to love it."

Many doctors I interviewed had to struggle and sacrifice to pursue their dream to enter medical school. They all told me that this gave them an appreciation for their chosen career and helped them be better students and physicians. Now, as they look back on their careers and accomplishments, they can echo the words of Dr. Fenner, "I killed it!"

DOCTORS AND TRAGEDY

Dr. Altimari, an experienced general surgeon, had tears in his eyes. I had never seen him cry before.

"What happened?" he said. "What happened?"

"I don't know," was my honest answer.

Dr. Altimari (Tony to his physician friends) had just operated on Peter Walton. Peter called me a week before with severe pain in his abdomen. I initially told him to come right over to the office, but when he called back and said he didn't think he could get out of the house because of the pain, I told him to go right to the emergency department. It was a good thing, because he was having an acute gallbladder attack with a gallstone stuck in the ducts that normally drain bile from the liver. He was already jaundiced (yellow) and had a bad infection related to the obstruction.

Peter was a longtime patient and one of my favorites. He was a World War II survivor. He served in intelligence, and his wife would kiddingly say that was the problem, "No intelligence." He was now in his declining years with a list of major medical problems that filled an entire page in his medical chart.

We stabilized him in the emergency department and admitted him to the hospital. I knew he would need his gallbladder removed, so I called my friend and well-respected surgeon, Tony.

"No problem," he said. "Get him 'tuned up,' and I'll take it out."

Over the next several days, we got Peter in the best medical shape possible. His cardiologist saw him for his heart, which was my greatest concern; an infectious disease specialist helped with antibiotic coverage; and a gastroenterologist removed the impacted gallstones through a minor nonsurgical procedure (endoscopy).

It was now the morning of surgery. Dr. Altimari walked into the room with the family.

"Are you ready?" he asked confidently. He knew the family well because he had operated on another family member, and they respected and trusted him.

"Sure am," said Peter.

"Are you certain he'll be all right?" asked his wife, Pat.

"This will be no problem," said Tony. "I'll be done in fifteen minutes, unless we have a problem, and then it may be twenty minutes." Everyone laughed, and the tension in the room evaporated with his light humor. As he spoke, he gently rubbed Peter's right foot. Dr. Altimari remembered that, as a child when he was undergoing a serious surgery, his physician gently touched his foot. That simple act of human contact calmed his fears and brought him peace. Now as a surgeon himself, he has continued this gentle touch for all of his preoperative patients.

As predicted, the surgery lasted only fifteen minutes, and Dr. Altimari met with Peter's son and wife and other family members in the patient waiting room.

"Everything went well," he said. "He's fine and will be out of recovery in about an hour."

However, as soon as Dr. Altimari left the hospital, Peter's blood pressure dropped. Pressors were started in an attempt to raise his blood pressure. Fluids were administered via IV, yet his blood pressure kept dropping. Then the oxygen level in his blood fell, and he became cold and sweaty. The pulmonary specialist in the ICU brought the "crash cart" into the room in order to put Peter on a ventilator to stop his rapid decline, but Peter, still in his right mind, refused. He had enough. His health had been deteriorating over the last year, and he did not want to prolong his life with heroic measures. He knew the end was near. A chaplain was called, and the family surrounded Peter's bed as a tearful prayer was offered. Not long afterward, Peter closed his eyes and his breathing became more and more shallow, until it stopped completely. Peter was dead.

I think many have the impression that an elderly patient's death would be relatively routine for physicians, but that is not the case. Long-term patients hold a special place in a doctor's heart, and their deaths are often like losing family members.

When I met with Dr. Altimari after Peter died, he was devastated.

"I loved that guy!" he kept saying.

Our emotions brought us both to tears.

"I don't think there was anything we could have done," I said. "It was his heart, an acute cardiac event or a myocardial infarction (heart attack). Tony, it wasn't your fault. You did everything right. He could not live with a sick gallbladder, and you had to take it out."

I think my words provided some comfort to the anguish he was feeling over thinking he contributed to the death of a dear friend.

That day, I realized again that good doctors, like Dr. Altimari, are human, that they really have emotions, and that they love the people they serve.

I had a similar relationship with my friend, neurosurgeon Dr. Doug Johnson. He was also my patient, but I almost never saw him professionally because he was never sick, until the day we found that he had gastric cancer.

Beth Johnson, who is the chief pathologist at our hospital, called me after she reviewed the surgical slides of her husband.

"Doug has a small nidus of cancer on the wall of his gallbladder. It looks like gastric."

There was a silence on the phone. I could tell Beth was emotional. We both knew that metastatic gastric cancer was almost never curable.

I didn't know what to say. After an uncomfortable silence I said, "Can I come over tonight?"

"Sure," she said. "Doug would like that."

I had strong mixed feelings as I walked up the steps to their beautiful home, a combination of sadness, anxiety, and determination to be as strong as I could be for them. Doug and Beth both greeted me. Beth had been crying and still had wet eyes. They asked me to come into the kitchen and sit down with them.

As I walked through the foyer and the family room I witnessed the pictures and memorabilia of a life of great accomplishment. The first thing that caught my eye was the large flag of the United States Marine Corps. Doug was very patriotic and had enlisted in the Navy and had achieved the rank of Captain. In the last year he left his successful practice as a neurosurgeon to serve as a doctor with a Marine detachment in the "Triangle of Death" in Iraq during the coalition invasion. He was on the front lines and was involved personally in firefights. In addition, he was responsible for stabilizing the wounded and for pronouncing the dead. None of my physician friends could believe he would take a year off to serve his country in such a dangerous position. But that was typical for Doug. He had great patriotism and felt that he owed his country for his freedoms. Fortunately he was uninjured in his service.

Then there were pictures of his children, Max and Abi. Max was a senior at the Naval Academy in Annapolis, Maryland, and Abi was an officer serving on an aircraft carrier on active duty. Then there was the picture of Doug crossing the finish line of one of his many marathons, including Boston. But that accomplishment was not enough for him. There was another picture of the Ironman triathlon, which he also mastered.

Inside the study where we sat and talked was the grand piano. Doug was an accomplished concert classical pianist, another one of the many talents of this Renaissance man. I really don't remember the words of our conversation that night, but I do remember the strong emotions we all felt. That was the beginning of a difficult journey that my good friend faced with surgery, chemotherapy, and progressive weakness.

One of Doug's wishes was that he witness the graduation of his son, Max, from the U.S. Naval Academy at Annapolis. The trip was difficult for him, and he needed to be pushed in a wheelchair with an oxygen cannula in his nose.

When the candidates were announced, Beth wheeled Doug over to the railing to see them file in. Max, in full dress uniform, saw his father immediately and, with a large contingent of his classmates, came right over to where Doug was sitting.

Then something remarkable happened. All the candidates present stood at attention and saluted Doug. With supreme effort, Captain Douglas Johnson rose slowly from his wheelchair, came to attention, and returned their salute. A more touching scene of love and devotion could not be imagined.

Doug lost his final battle soon after returning from that trip.

He survived only four months after the diagnosis was made, but he taught me something in that short time. He taught me to live life to the fullest, to have dignity and honor even to the end, and to be true to what you believe, the essence of the Marine Corps motto, *Semper Fidelis*, always faithful.

DOCTORS WITNESS THE MYSTERIES OF DEATH AND DYING

"How dare you violate my wishes [to let my son die]," said a distraught mother to Dr. Leyva early in her career as a pediatrician in charge of the pediatric intensive care unit. It was this interaction that started Dr. Leyva on the path to become what she is today, a palliative care physician. (Palliative care physicians specialize in caring for patients with serious or terminal illnesses.)

Just that morning, she admitted Jonathan, an unfortunate ten-year-old boy, to her ICU with an aspiration pneumonia. Jonathan was born with severe brain damage and was now at the end of his life, with repeated admissions for pneumonia related to aspirating his own secretions, since he could not swallow properly. Dr. Leyva recognized that he was lacking oxygen and simply put on a BIPAP device (a noninvasive breathing machine). This caused the angry outburst from a frustrated mother.

"He has been in and out of the hospital every two weeks with severe pneumonias. He cannot function without maximal support in his pediatric nursing home and will not survive the year. If he lives through this illness, he will only face dying from another pneumonia. Please, let God take him!" she sobbed.

Jonathan did ultimately die of an aspiration pneumonia, but Dr. Leyva was touched so deeply by his illness and the anguished mother that it started her on a journey to find a more loving way to care for terminally ill pediatric patients. Over the next weeks, she contacted every children's hospital and clinic in Chicago looking for advice from pediatric palliative care experts, but there were none. The specialty was in its infancy.

When she posted Jonathan's story on a physician blog, it was "coincidently" seen by Dr. David Sine, an early pioneer in palliative care from Rady Children's Hospital in San Diego, California. His advice: "Drop everything and come out immediately to learn from what we are doing here." And that is exactly what Dr. Leyva did. Within weeks, she was on a plane flying from Chicago to San Diego to study under Dr. Sine and the leading institution at the time.

There she learned the importance of helping seriously ill patients achieve their goals in life. This became a recurrent theme for her. "It seems that every terminal patient has something to look forward to, some goal that they want to accomplish. It became my job to move heaven and earth to try to accomplish that goal."

She remembers her experience with a fourteen-year-old girl in the San Diego hospice unit who had never been to the beach. Visiting the beach was her ultimate goal, but she was too ill to travel, so Dr. Leyva and the staff brought the beach to her. They carried in bags of sand, fans for the breeze and even a real lifeguard in uniform (bathing suit). When they brought the dying young girl outside to see the scene with the ocean off in the distance, not only did she cry tears of joy, but every one of the staff cried with her.

Dr. Leyva has become a preeminent palliative care physician in the western suburbs of Chicago. She is living her dream of helping children, and now adults, achieve their goals and live their last days with pride and dignity. She related some interesting observations of patients at the end of life. "People who are near death often have experiences that are beyond this world, and they are universally positive." She is convinced that when people are dying, they are sometimes comforted by loved ones from the other side. She remembers watching a terminal ninety-year-old woman get all dressed up in imaginary clothes and jewelry so that she would be pretty enough for her departed friends.

I have personally used Dr. Leyva to assist with the final days and weeks of multiple patients. She has been instrumental in helping my patients achieve their final wishes and in helping families cope with the devastating loss. But, most importantly for me, she helped me cope with the loss of a special patient and neurosurgeon, Dr. Doug Johnson.

John Saran, MD, a fellow internist, related a touching story of a middle-aged man with metastatic cancer who had gone through chemotherapy and radiation therapy, but after multiple treatments had failed everything and was now dying. He knew his prognosis and wanted to be at home. His wishes were accomplished through his hospice team, who provided nursing, medical care, and equipment at home to allow him to be well attended outside the hospital. Toward the end, from his hospital bed, he kept looking over to a place in his living room. After some time, he asked his wife if she saw it also. "Why no," she said. "What are you seeing?"

"There are three young women in white dresses dancing with each other in a circle. They are smiling and happy. What do you think they are doing here?" he asked.

His wife, who had a strong faith, answered in an amazingly matter-of-fact way, "What you are seeing are angels who have come down to take you to heaven."

The answer provided great comfort for her husband who, still feeling the responsibility for his family and children, replied, "Well, I'll take care of things on the other side if you can take care of things on earth."

"That's a deal," she replied, holding back her tears.

He smiled and closed his eyes, and, as he left his mortal sphere, he was accompanied, I am certain, by the three young angels that only he could see, dancing in his living room.

FINAL THOUGHTS

I have spent three years listening to doctors tell me of their extraordinary experiences. Some interviews took place in the doctors' lounge in our hospital over a quick breakfast or lunch, some in doctor's homes, some over the phone, some by text, some at nurses' stations, and some while walking to a meeting or a patient's room. We all tend to be so busy that I caught up with physicians wherever I could. Many of the stories I heard were so miraculous that I had chills and goose bumps, and many brought me to tears. I still get misty even retelling some of their remarkable experiences.

I also listened to doctors talk about their lives and what was important to them. These revelations made me proud to associate with such exemplary women and men. I learned that there is still good in this turbulent world, that there are people who care about others, and who try to help someone in need every day. I learned that there are still individuals who do not mind working hard and sacrificing to achieve a worthwhile goal. I learned that even though physicians value their careers, that family values rank even higher. And I learned that the majority of the physicians interviewed were spiritual beyond what I ever imagined and that they knew there was a power beyond our simple existence, a power who loves us unconditionally and who participates in our lives more than we realize, a power that many of my fellow physicians and I call God.

I have been changed by my interactions with these doctors. My faith has been strengthened, my determination to be a better person has been reawakened, and I have a new optimism for the future. But most importantly, I have learned to recognize the little (and sometimes big) coincidences that help direct my path for the good. And I have learned that many of these "divine coincidences" are often not coincidental at all.

Afterword: Divine Coincidences

~

I began this book with the story of how I, like many other doctors, became a physician through a combination of hard work, sleep deprivation, and determination. But I left out the most interesting part of the story, how a divine coincidence made my entire medical career possible.

I was enrolled in organic chemistry at Aurora University, the last medical school prerequisite. I was on track. I had been out of college for two years trying for acceptance into a medical school, and, with a growing family to support, I calculated I could not afford to wait one more year to get in. If not the coming year, I would have to get a "real" job and give up my ambition to become a doctor.

As I sat in the classroom awaiting the professor, I was optimistic about my plans and thankful that Aurora was so close to my job in the same city. The other school offering organic chemistry at night was Roosevelt University in downtown Chicago, sixty-five miles from my home.

My train of thought was interrupted when the classroom door suddenly popped open. A young professor in a light brown suit entered with a distressed look on his face. He did not sit down but stood in front of the class, which consisted of only three other students.

"I'm afraid I have bad news," he said.

I felt the butterflies in my stomach.

"We have to cancel the class since there are not enough students enrolled."

I quickly looked around to see if anyone else had come in, and then down the hall through the open door, hoping to see if anyone was waiting outside. No one. There were just four of us. Now I know why there were so many dark green organic chemistry books in the bookstore. No one bought them. I wanted to cry. I wondered if my medical school career was over.

I graduated from college with a major in economics but now decided to go back to medical school. For as long as I could remember, I wanted to become a physician, but, in college, I became disillusioned with the science classes that were required and changed my major to economics, my second love. The tipping point occurred in the embryology lab late one evening before a major test. Most of the class was there, eyes glued to the optics of the microscopes studying slides of tiny animal embryos sectioned at least one hundred times. I was struggling to determine where the notochord began and where it ended when one of my female classmates leaned over.

"Isn't this exciting!" she said. "I heard that this is exactly what medical school will be like."

I wanted to throw up. If this was what medical school was going to be about, I wanted nothing to do with it. The next day I became an economist.

Now I was out of school working as a computer and accounting representative, just as computers were coming into the market. I hated it. It really didn't seem to make any difference in the overall scheme of life if a bank or corporation bought a machine from me or from one of my competitors. I was tired of trying to sell someone on one of the minor differences our products had over one of my equally qualified competitors. On my drive back home from an upset school district customer in Sycamore, Illinois, I had my epiphany. I would go back to medical school and fulfill my childhood dream. I was now married, and I would speak with my wife, Joan, about putting me through school. Luckily she was incredibly supportive, so I was on my way.

We sat down and began an intricate plan that would take two years to complete and then I could enroll in medical school (if I was accepted). Because of my economics major, I did not have all the prerequisites, and the major one was organic chemistry. In order to stay on my plan I would need to enroll now to finish the yearlong course. But suddenly, my class was canceled.

After regaining my composure, I determined I would suffer the long sixty-five-mile commute to Roosevelt University where the only other class was offered at night. That would be a trek, but I decided that if I had to do it to get into school, I would drive there in the morning and enroll.

The next day, I awoke filled with hope. I called my employer and made some excuse for taking the morning off and drove immediately to Roosevelt University in Chicago. The gray stone building sat on a major corner on Michigan Avenue overlooking the lake. I was impressed with the mosaic floor in the lobby with scenes from past civilizations. The lobby was bustling with last-minute enrollment and class changes, but I found the line I needed, and, after what seemed like an eternity, I was in the front.

"What can I help you with?" said the weary counselor.

"I need to enroll in the evening organic chemistry class," I explained to her.

"I'm so sorry," she said. "That class is totally filled. In fact the demand was so great that we opened up a second class, and that is also filled, and we have a waiting list of twenty students."

"You don't understand," I said. "I need to enroll in this class or I won't be able to get into medical school. There must be something I can do!"

"I'm very sorry," she said. "Everyone on the waiting list is trying to get into a professional school. You're not alone."

Somehow, that didn't make me feel any better.

"Is there someone I could talk to?" I asked.

"The only person who can authorize additional students is the professor teaching the class."

Great, I thought, another ray of hope for my fading medical school career. By this point I was desperate.

"How do I meet with the professor?" I asked.

"Third floor, room 303, and ask for Professor Rubin."

I ran up the stairs so fast that I stumbled. Room 303 was filled with waiting students, I imagined with the same problem I had. I went right up to the secretary and in between my panting from running, I asked if I could see Professor Rubin for just a minute.

"I'm sorry," she said. "Professor Rubin is very busy preparing for the start of classes tomorrow. He can probably meet with you sometime next week."

Now I was almost in tears. I think the poor secretary could feel my pain.

"Okay," she said. "If you can make it a quick meeting, you can go in after the professor is finished speaking with Professor Johnson, who is teaching the other organic chemistry class." She escorted me to a little anteroom just outside his office. The door to his office was wood paneled with a large frosted glass window, which easily transmitted the sounds from inside the office. I could not help but overhear the conversation taking place inside the room.

"I don't know what we are going to do," said one professor. "We now have two full classes for organic chemistry and a waiting list of twenty potential students, and we only have books for one class and cannot possibly get the books we need. The publisher is out and none are available from any of the schools I called."

"We can't cancel the second class!" said the second professor. "I'll make a few more calls and speak with the dean, but we have to do something today!"

Then the door handle turned and the second professor left the room and Dr. Rubin, who seemed to be very distracted, motioned for me to come in.

What I blurted out at the time is now gone from my memory, but Professor Rubin listened politely to my pleading, and then told me exactly what the registrar had indicated about the waiting list and that he was sorry. He reached out and shook my hand as a parting gesture. My medical career was over. This was it. What a way to end.

As I turned to walk out there was a flash of inspiration! Yesterday I was at the Aurora University bookstore where there were so many organic chemistry books they were falling off three shelves. *Dare I say this?* I had never done anything like this before, but these were desperate times that called for desperate measures. My life was on the line! I turned around.

"Professor Rubin," I stuttered, "if I can get enough books for your second class, would you let me enroll?"

I had his attention! His raised his eyebrows. "Could you get thirty books?" he asked.

"More," I said.

My heart was beating in my throat. The long silence was deafening. I waited and waited. Then he looked me in the eye.

"Yes," he said.

I had done it!

Nothing could stop me now. I explained to him where the books were, and he asked his secretary to call the Aurora University Bookstore.

At the time, I really didn't think it was much more than a coincidence being outside that professor's office at the very moment that they were discussing a problem only I could solve. But in retrospect, I know I was there so I could finish my prerequisites and enroll in medical school. That was the beginning of a series of miraculous events that guided me through my medical training. But it took the perspective of time for me to be able to connect the dots and realize the gift I had been given.

DIVINE COINCIDENCES

Many of the stories in this book have contained what I call "divine coincidences," events and people inexplicably coming together with amazing results. Dr. Johnson, who had just learned of a new surgical technique that he could employ on his friend. Dr. Mendenhall, who was miraculously brought to a nearby hospital to operate on the broken arms of a friend's daughter. Dr. Saran, who rejected numerous flight and vacation plans, leading to an airline where he was needed to deliver a baby. Only in retrospect were they able to recognize the connections.

As my story about enrolling in medical school illustrates, not all divine coincidences involve life-or-death situations. One advantage of growing older is my ability to look back and recognize an unseen hand directing my path. What many might call "coincidence" I deem "providence." Recognizing that providence fills me with awe and gratitude.

Why did I feel compelled to share these physicians' stories? Because so often we take life for granted. Because in the press of ordinary, daily life, we forget that amazing things are happening all around us. Because sometimes we need a reminder that the physical world and the physical body can point to another, unseen reality.

That is the physician's untold story.

About the Doctors

~⌢

Anthony Altimari, MD

Dr. Altimari is a general surgeon in group practice in Wheaton, Illinois. He graduated from Northwestern University and attended the Chicago Medical School. He completed a five-year residency in general surgery at Loyola University. He is always at the cutting edge (sorry for the bad pun) and was one of the first in the area to champion laparoscopic surgery.

Tony loves music, and everyone knows that he regularly plays "gigs" with his rock band.

"How did you get started?" I asked.

"It started with guitar Mass," he said.

"What?"

"Guitar Mass. It's when the Catholic Church changed to having guitars play during Mass. The nuns taught me to play in sixth grade (but not rock), and I have been playing ever since. I had a band in grade school, high school, college, medical school, residency, and now. We'll play for anyone, and we frequently even get paid."

But the last few engagements were for charity, including his last, which was to raise funds for a young man with a serious spinal cord injury. Tony plays the guitar, but he looks forward to relieving his frustrations by playing the drums when the drummer doesn't show up. He also plays the piano "and anything else I can get my hands on."

I asked what was most important to him and, without hesitation, he replied, "My family. My life has been a balancing act between being a busy, successful general surgeon and being with my family. The last of my three children, my baby, who was just born yesterday, is now going to college on Sunday. It's hard to believe. Every night we play 'gotch ya.' That's where we chase like wild men around the house and try to be the last to tag the other person. It's stupid, but I'll miss that. I'll miss him."

I know he will, because his priorities are in the right place, and they always have been. That's just the way he is.

Fred Bollhoffer, MD

Dr. Bollhoffer is an emergency department physician at Northwestern Medicine Central DuPage Hospital in Winfield, Illinois. He graduated from the University of Illinois College of Medicine and completed his residency in emergency medicine at Lutheran General Hospital in Park Ridge, Illinois.

I discovered during our interviews that Dr. Bollhoffer and I were in different classes at the same medical school at the same time, although we never met there. We met years later on the phone. Our conversation went something like this.

Phone rings. "Hello," I said.

"Hi, Dr. Kolbaba, this is the CDH ER. Please hold for Dr. Bollhoffer," said the nurse.

"Hi, Scott," said a cheery voice, "This is Fred Bollhoffer."

I looked at the clock. Three in the morning. "Hi...Fred."

"Scott, I have one of your patients brought in by ambulance, Alice Rogers. Do you remember her?"

Then a silence. I suddenly felt an elbow in my side, and my wife whispered, "Wake up!"

"Yes," I said. "I just saw Alice in the office. What happened?"

"Chest pain. Doesn't sound like anything serious, normal EKG, chest X-ray and troponin, but I think we should watch her overnight."

"Sounds fine," I said. "If you can tuck her in, I'll see her in the a.m."

Alice was fine in the morning, and I ultimately did meet Fred, and we have become friends, despite his many untimely calls.

Dr. Bollhoffer declares that his greatest accomplishment in life is not his career, but his family. "What is the point of having children if your main goal is not to set them on the correct path? It is the circle of life and the circle of humanity. That is what is missing in our society today, interest in our children and in our values."

When we discussed the story of his patient's vision of deceased relatives (chapter twelve), he told me, "Experiences like this one make me realize that there is something more than what we experience on a day-to-day basis in this life. If you talk to anyone in the ER, they will have a story like this to tell. It's in our literature. Everyone here knows that there are things that we cannot explain, that there is something more."

John R. Born, DO

Dr. Born practices family medicine in Wheaton, Illinois, and has been my only partner since we joined our practices in 2007. It's hard to believe that we have been together that long, and I can't remember ever having a disagreement. He graduated from the Chicago College of Osteopathic Medicine and served his residency at the same institution.

He has a special interest in medical executive leadership and went to night school to obtain his MBA from Benedictine University in Lisle, Illinois. Applying his skills, he was elected medical staff president at Central DuPage Hospital in Winfield, Illinois, serving over seven hundred physicians. This is a one-year position, and I remember some painful mornings when he would have one or two meetings before morning office hours and need to make rounds at four in the morning to fit everything in.

One of his three children is starting college, and one starts in a year. His first son did so well on his college entrance exams (perfect scores) and grade point average (straight A's) that he was offered multiple scholarships as an entering freshman in the engineering school at the University of Illinois. In fact, John (J. B. to his friends) received a call from the dean indicating that they would have to take back some of the scholarships since his son would otherwise be earning considerably more than the cost of his education.

J. B. absolutely loves cars, and his favorite is his Corvette Stingray. Unfortunately, it is aging, and he can no longer find repair parts. He has held off on buying a new one in order to save for college expenses. Now that his son is well situated and his other son is not far behind, I am looking forward to a ride in a new Corvette!

Gordon D. Brown, MD

Dr. Brown is an interventional radiologist practicing in a suburb of Salt Lake City, Utah. He graduated from the University of Utah School of Medicine and did his internship at the University of Utah and residency at UCLA Medical Center.

When he first started in practice, interventional radiology was in its infancy, and many hospitals did not support that specialty. I kid him about not being a "real" doctor, but his specialty has now become a mainstay of every hospital. His job is to do angiography, open up blood vessels and biopsy organs and tumors without surgery by placing catheters and needles (of course with anesthesia) in multiple locations in the body, including the liver, kidney, and even pancreas.

He admits to being a certified (not certifiable) do-gooder. During the Vietnam War, he joined the Public Health Service to provide care wherever he was needed. He was assigned to a Coast Guard cutter off the coast of Vietnam. In that assignment, he boldly traveled from village to village with garbage cans filled with supplies and performed random acts of kindness and healing wherever he went. One memorable case was a beautiful young Vietnamese girl who had been shot in the foot. Dr. Brown offered to X-ray her foot at their ship. The girl's father agreed to the plan, and they carried her twenty miles through the swamps of the Mekong Delta to get to the ship. There the X-ray showed that a bone was fractured, but there were no lead fragments remaining. Dr. Brown was able to bandage the wound and leave enough supplies for the loving father to care for his injured daughter until she healed.

The turning point in Dr. Brown's career came during a conversation with his memorable biology teacher, Dr. Thomas

Bahler. Dr. Brown told him of his interest in biology and that he might consider medicine as a career.

"You can do it if you really want it," he remembered Dr. Bahler saying, and that was when he made his decision. "And I never looked back."

Dr. Bahler was so influential to such a large number of students that a scholarship was created in his name, which Dr. Brown gratefully supports to this day.

"What is most important to you?" I asked.

"Faith means everything to me, and my family is what it's all about," he told me.

Patrick C. Fenner, MD

Dr. Fenner is a cardiologist in practice in the western suburbs of Chicago. He graduated from Wayne State University School of Medicine in Detroit, and he did his residency in internal medicine at Butterworth Hospital in Grand Rapids, Michigan. He completed his fellowship in cardiology at Rush-Presbyterian St. Luke's Medical Center in Chicago.

Although Patrick loves the practice of cardiology, his other passion has always been sports, both as a spectator and participant. In fact, an experience in basketball became the major tipping point that changed his life. He was competing for a position as a freshman on the Michigan Tech basketball team. During the tryout, he recognized that he would not be a starter, but he knew that if he could beat out Ron Janson, he would have a place as a regular sub on the team. Ron knew that too, and he wanted the spot badly. Patrick knew that Ron was not as experienced and probably not as talented, but what he lacked in talent, he made up in heart. He ran between stations; he dove for the ball. "It was obvious that he wanted it more than I did, and I let up on the pedal. To this day I don't know why, and Ron made the team—I did not."

"How did that make you feel?" I asked.

"I was devastated," he said. "It made me feel terrible, and I never wanted to feel that way again, so I determined that I would *never, ever* give up on something I wanted. I knew that I might not succeed at everything I tried, but I would make sure I did my very best. And I have."

Dr. Fenner enrolled in medical school after years of rejections. He ultimately secured a cardiology fellowship reserved for only the brightest internal medicine residency graduates.

In his leisure time he climbed Mount Kilimanjaro in Africa, and his most recent conquest was a major bicycle ride from Dubuque, Iowa, to Kenosha, Wisconsin, 175 miles in one day. He did it in eleven hours!

He has imparted his experiences to the loves of his life, his daughters Payton and Piper. They are also athletic and accomplished skiers. When Payton was eight and standing at the top of a mountain, facing a run that looked like an elevator shaft nearly straight down, she asked her companion, a former Olympic skier, if she was afraid. She replied, "You know, fear is just lack of confidence. You need to point your skis, and go down like you own it!" And Payton did.

Just like her father who "owns" everything he does.

David K. Gieser, MD

Dr. Gieser is an ophthalmologist in private practice in Wheaton, Illinois. His subspecialty is glaucoma, and he is particularly interested in the use of medications for the treatment of eye disorders. He graduated from the University of Illinois College of Medicine and did his residency at the Eye and Ear Infirmary of the University of Illinois in Chicago. He completed further training in glaucoma at Washington University in St. Louis.

The tipping point in his life came when he believes a faculty prayer healed his ruptured kidney, the story he included in this book. "That event changed my life," he told me. "After that, I knew there was a God and that there is power in prayer. It also gave me a desire to help others whenever I could." And that he has done throughout his life (another do-gooder!).

Dr. Gieser has traveled extensively in central Africa, teaching doctors in multiple countries. In addition he participates in his local community by serving as Chairman of the Board of Trustees of Wheaton College, the alma mater of evangelist Billy Graham and one of the most prestigious small faith-based liberal arts colleges in the United States.

His son, observing his father's passion for helping others, now oversees educational programs for seventeen graduate schools in Africa, and his other son, an Army Ranger officer, has been responsible for the interment of military heroes at Arlington National Cemetery.

Despite all of his great credentials and laudits, he still sees his lowly internist, me, to perform my routine eye exams.

Stephen J. Graham, MD

Dr. Graham graduated from Temple University and attended the University of Pittsburgh School of Medicine. He completed his residency in emergency medicine at the University of Illinois.

He admits that there were two major turning points in his life. The first was when his father was killed in an accident when he was just two years old. His mother struggled to provide for the family, and he remembers not having as many opportunities as many of his friends. That may be why he now is the ultimate husband and father. "I wanted to give my kids the opportunities I never had," he told me.

He has four children, including twins. He coaches his children's football and basketball teams and teaches his children hunting and fishing, and their vacations are both educational and adventurous. His most memorable was to the Galapagos Islands, where he and the children found the animals "incredible."

His other turning point was an inspirational conversation with a nun at his grade school. He talks about it in the conclusion of this book.

In his spare time, Dr. Graham uses hockey as a stress reliever. He plays in a competitive adult league, and he still has his own front teeth!

Dr. Graham has five-star ratings by his patients and the respect of all of his colleagues. He even apologizes to me when he calls with an emergency admission in the middle of the night.

Stephen E. Heim, MD

Dr. Heim practices orthopedic surgery with a specialty in spinal surgery in Wheaton, Illinois. He has been in private practice for over twenty-five years. His training was at Northwestern University in Chicago for medical school, residency, and spine fellowship.

He then served his country as a Naval surgeon for nine years. He told me he frequently treated airmen who were injured when their parachutes didn't open. I was surprised that anyone could survive such a mishap, but, evidently, if the ground was soft with the spring rains, many would sink to their knees but survive. Part of his service was also as a flight surgeon on some dangerous missions that still remain "top secret."

Even though he became a grandfather for the first time this year, Dr. Heim keeps himself in top military condition and can still do one thousand push-ups and one thousand sit-ups.

One of his great "stress relievers" is auto racing. He belongs to a Porsche racing club and regularly races during the summer. In one of his most spectacular races, he ran off the track at high speed, breaking through a fourteen-inch wooden guard rail. Even though he sustained only minor injuries, that would definitely not be my idea of stress relief!

I asked if he had an explanation for his story of saving an unknown skier in Colorado. "I don't attend a regular church," he told me, "but after an event like I went through, how could you not believe in the Man above!"

John A. Heitzler, MD

Dr. Heitzler practiced obstetrics and gynecology in Wheaton, Illinois, for thirty-seven years until his much-deserved retirement in 1998. He graduated from Loyola University Stritch School of Medicine and did his residency at the same institution.

In the local community he still has celebrity status, and, wherever he goes, a mother will invariably run up to him and thank him for his successful delivery of one or more of her children as she scrambles through her purse to show him multiple pictures of her now grown and accomplished children. In fact, my wife is one of those women, since Dr. Heitzler (Jack) delivered our Nathan in 1980, and yes, Nathan is successful and "perfect in every way." I asked him if he was bothered by all the attention, and he told me that he puts up with it. Joan, his wife, however, told me on the side, "He *loves* it!"

Jack has enjoyed flying small planes throughout his life and took his family (his first love) all around the country. One of their most harrowing flights was from Beaver Island in Lake Michigan. A sudden cloudburst hit the lake while they were flying back to Chicago, and they had to make an emergency landing in Door County, Wisconsin. The rain was coming down in blinding sheets as Dr. Heitzler attempted to land the plane in a farm field, until they heard the mooing. Looking out the side windows, the children discover a herd of frightened cows running in all directions. Dr. Heitzler pulled up as hard as he could to avoid playing dodge ball with the poor cows below, only to find that they were heading for a crash landing in an apple orchard at the end of the field. By great luck, the plane remained airborne through the apple branches, and the only damage was an apple lodged in the wing's landing light!

As an obstetrician, Dr. Heitzler had a reputation for regularly performing miracles. He was too humble to tell me this story, but his wife told me he was called by a younger obstetrician to help deliver a second twin. While running to the delivery room, he said a silent prayer that God would guide his hands, his routine before every delivery. When he scrubbed and entered the delivery room, the unborn baby was in distress, and he would need to do an emergency Cesarean section or lose the baby. The mother, a nurse herself, refused the surgery. A hush came over the nursing staff and students now crowded into the delivery room. The eerie silence was broken when one of the senior nurses quietly whispered to the other, "Watch the old fox do this!" And within a few minutes, the second baby was delivered, without surgery, alive and screaming!

In his retirement, the "old fox" still flies as a copilot with his friends and still acknowledges a thank you from a grateful mother.

Michael I. Hussey, MD

Dr. Hussey is retiring after an impressive fifty-two
tice of obstetrics and gynecology. "And I still love
me.

He graduated from Notre Dame University an
Loyola University Stritch School of Medicine. He
residency at Cook County Hospital in Chicago. H
medicine rubbed off on his children, three of whom
cians in his same specialty. In addition, two other ch
in medical-related fields.

He served in the Public Health Service, where he authored
a portion of the Surgeon General's report that initially linked
smoking to cancer. He demonstrated the effectiveness of Pap
smears in screening for cervical cancer and was also instrumental in setting up clinics at military bases to serve indigent
populations.

His life has been one of service. His story about his mission trip to the Philippines (chapter sixteen) was just one of
multiple trips over his lifetime to treat underserved populations around the world. He even saves dogs. His present pet is
a beagle, the eighth family dog, each rescued from an animal
shelter.

When I asked him what he is most grateful for, he quickly
answered, "The opportunity to practice medicine." I am grateful too, since he delivered our fourth child, Ian, who was high
risk and weighed only four pounds, twelve ounces at birth. I
think I forgot to tell you, Dr. Hussy, that Ian is now six feet
four inches and wears size fourteen shoes. He also does deliveries, but, as a vet, he delivers mostly dogs and cats.

Douglas Johnson, MD, PhD

Dr. Johnson, neurosurgeon, died after a four-month battle with gastric cancer, just after he told his touching story about saving the life of a fellow neurosurgeon (chapter twenty). He was truly a Renaissance man who became proficient as a great surgeon (he operated on my neck), concert pianist, marathon and Ironman participant, and soldier. He served with a Marine detachment in the "Triangle of Death" in Iraq.

I think one of the most touching tributes and testaments to his character was written as a eulogy to his fellow Marines by his commanding officer. I have included it here.

All,

I bring this update with a heavy heart, and for my Marine brothers and friends please brace yourselves, but Dr. Doug Johnson, Captain Doug Johnson USNR passed away on Tues, surrendering his fight with abdominal cancer and going home to his God.

Doug and I had been communicating since his diagnosis last year, and much like the bond between warriors, we shared a bond that can truly only be understood among cancer fighters. Through his battle, Doug was the epitome of dignity, strength, and LOVE. What always struck me, and will always stick with me is how when we would talk, what Doug most talked about was not his cancer or his struggle, but his children, and his wife. And he despised how hard the struggle was on them. Again, it was just another reminder of the Doug Johnson I know: "others not self!"

For those on my support list who may not have known Doug, let me summarize. Doug was a very successful neurosurgeon practicing in the Chicago area. He joined the US Navy Reserve in his *fifties* following the attacks of September 11, 2001, because, as he said, "I owe this country." Sacrificing millions of dollars, Doug deployed with us as part of 2/24 during our deployment in the Triangle of Death in 2004/2005. He was one of our two surgeons and as such was critical to the care of our Marines. Doug was the first to handle the bodies of our beloved KIAs upon their return to FOB [forward operating base] St. Michael, and the reverence with which he executed his duties was purely magical. He would pass the bodies off to the care of Sergeant Major Payne, who would stand diligently by their side until the bodies had been placed on the Angel Flight for the journey home.

I was relentless as the Commander in my requirement for the wearing of all issued armor anytime outside a hardened structure, and Doug Johnson, all 5'6" of him and his full 130 lbs, would run PT around FOB St. Michael, EVERY day, in shorts, running shoes, his body armor and helmet, his issued shotgun, and the largest smile you have ever seen in your life. That is what I always do, and always will remember about Doug Johnson, that freaking INCESSANT smile ... hell, a smirkish grin really. He was always smiling. He loved every second of every experience he was involved in. He was a total pain in my ass. He was constantly darkening my doorway with that never-ending smile and pestering me to "go forward." He wanted to be out with the Marines, and he wanted to be where the bullets were flying and were the roads would disintegrate in a millisecond into a powerful IED explosion. He was, quite frankly, a little bit nuts! One day I pulled him into my office, shut the door, and said, "Doc, do you have any idea how much of a pain in my ass you are?" He smiled that freaking smile, and said, "Yes, sir, I do ... and that is my plan. Eventually you will kick me off this FOB." I laughed, thought to myself this guy fifteen years my senior and a freaking neuro-surgeon calls me Sir in the middle of a stone age war - God does have a sense of humor - and then I said, "Seriously man, I am just a badge-wearing, gun-toting Trooper ... how much money are you losing by being here?" He laughed and stated that it was no big deal, and so I a little more emphatically (for those who know mean read a little more emphatically as with several F bombs) asked him again. He looked at me, still smiling of course, and said, "Well, let's put it this way, what I will make this year from the Navy won't even account for what I owe a year in malpractice insurance." I said, "Holy s—"! He laughed, kept that smile on his face, and said, "So when can I go forward?" I said "Doc, get the f— out of my office!" He walked out smiling ear to ear, and I immediately went to the S-3 and said make arrangements for Doc Johnson to be on the next resup-ply to Fox Company and let MoMann know he will be spending a few days with them.

That was Doug Johnson ... the smile, the never-ending, incessant, sometimes downright aggravating smile. I have often pondered why he smiled so much ... and thanks to my own cancer diagnosis, I learned the answer, and the answer lies in what I said about Doug earlier: LOVE. He LOVED his sailors, he LOVED his Marines, he LOVED his country, he LOVED doing his duty. In getting to be around those he loved, doing what he loved, he could not suppress the smile of his inner joy. AND I AM SO D— GLAD HE COULDN'T, BECAUSE THAT MAGNIFICANT B— WAS A BEAM OF JOY IN WHAT COULD HAVE BEEN AN OTHERWISE UGLY ENVIRONMENT.

Doug Johnson was successful in every way we measure a man: he was a neurosurgeon, a Captain in the Navy, a philanthropist, and a great guy. But, more importantly, Doug Johnson was a success in the ways we should measure a man. He was a phenomenal husband and father. He adored his wife and he lived for his kids. What does it say about a man as financially well to do as he was that his children have gone on to become United States Naval officers? It says far more than this uneducated moron ever could. Doug Johnson would be sold short if he were not counted a warrior, for he was. A true warrior for his country and for his family.

Doug Johnson was a man that I proudly and unabashedly say, I loved! I loved him, and he set examples for me of manhood that I will never achieve. I loved him and my heart is shattered for his wife and children, and my eyes weep openly for their loss. I loved him and I have not even a second's doubt that the Doug Johnson smile was very recently emulated, emulated by the only other person who could truly understand the smile that comes from such a satisfied love, Jesus Christ, as he welcomed him into his Kingdom.

I loved Doug Johnson, and I will miss him. Doug Johnson was many things to many people, and the world will be a lesser place for his departure, but for me, and just being totally selfish here, I will be a lesser man without him, because Doug Johnson was MY FRIEND! God bless you, my brother, go gently into that light, and know your family has an entire battalion of the world's finest Marines to lean on!

Mark A. Smith
Colonel USMCR
Lieutenant Colonel, ISP

Richard Jorgensen, MD

Dr. Jorgensen graduated from Loyola University Stritch School of Medicine and served a residency in general surgery at Loyola, and then a fellowship in vascular surgery at the Medical College of Wisconsin. He was in private practice as a general surgeon until he retired in 2008. In fact, I trusted this highly respected surgeon to remove my wife's appendix and all lived, including the husband. He loved his career and medicine, but after developing a severe allergy to the plastics used in the operating room, he was forced to retire.

Still wanting to save lives every day, he ran for county coroner and was elected. He has always been politically active, particularly since his wife became a circuit judge. They both rose to national attention when she tried a case involving the sale of a baseball card.

You didn't think coroners save lives? They usually don't, but Rich—horrified at the large number of young people who died from heroin overdoses in DuPage County, Illinois— initiated a program where every policeman, fireman, and paramedic could be equipped with the immediate antidote for heroin, Narcan. When injected shortly after a respiratory arrest from heroin, the victim would immediately awaken. To date, he has been responsible for saving over sixty adolescents and young adults from an untimely death. Yes, even physician coroners can be do-gooders!

Scott J. Kolbaba, MD

Dr. Kolbaba is an internist in private practice in Wheaton, Illinois. He graduated from the University of Illinois College of Medicine with honors and did his residency at Rush-Presbyterian Medical Center in Chicago and at the Mayo Clinic in Rochester, Minnesota. He has been awarded membership in the Alpha Omega Alpha Honor Medical Society and has been featured in *Chicago* magazine as a "Top Doctor" in internal medicine.

His friends accuse him of specializing in "big." Being an only child, he now has a big family of seven children and nine grandchildren. "I wouldn't give up any of them, at least most of the time!" His Newfoundland puppy is already one hundred thirty pounds and growing, and he likes to fly kites. Yes, only the big ones. At sixteen square meters, his bright orange and green kiteboarding kite was his favorite until it pulled him and his neighbor off the ground with a gentle breeze. They both dropped off before they ended up in the clouds. He still doesn't understand why his neighbor won't help with his kite hobby anymore.

Following the same theme in his garden, Dr. Kolbaba has grown Atlantic Giant pumpkins and is the proud winner of the Sycamore, Illinois, pumpkin-growing contest two years running. The first time was a surprise, but, the next year, the family invited all their friends to the festivities, which started with the cord cutting in the pumpkin patch by an experienced gynecologist. A caravan of obnoxious horn-blowing cars followed the flatbed truck carrying the precious pumpkin to the contest, where they were pronounced the winner again with a trophy and a cash prize (fifteen dollars).

Like many of his friends, Dr. Kolbaba considers himself a card-carrying "do-gooder." His family helps support an orphanage in Romania supervised by REMM (Romanian Evangelical Medical Mission), where they adopted two of their children. His ultimate goal is to provide enough support to help many more orphans and street children.

His family is relieved that his three-year sojourn to complete this book is over, but, as he looks up from his laptop Dr. Kolbaba has a wry smile. Thinking of book number two...
Bigger?

Ileana M. Leyva, MD

Dr. Leyva started as a pediatrician but converted her practice to hospice and palliative care medicine. She completed her undergraduate education at the University of Miami in Florida and medical school at Central University of the East in the Dominican Republic. She did residency training in pediatrics at Lutheran General Hospital in Park Ridge, Illinois.

Her father was a prominent Cuban senator who found himself on an execution list when Fidel Castro took over the country. That was a real incentive to leave all their possessions and flee to Miami, Florida, where Mr. Leyva took whatever work he could get to support the family. Dr. Leyva cherished her childhood and her Cuban heritage (including the great food) and never realized her family was poor until she was older.

Since she came from such humble beginnings, I asked how she achieved her success.

"My dad drilled his work ethic into me," she told me. "He worked two jobs into his eighties and told me that the only obstacle to your success is yourself. I learned that if I wanted something bad enough and was willing to work, I could achieve it. I went to medical school in the Dominican Republic because we could not afford American medical schools. One year, we did not have enough money for school, and I was about to drop out and get a job when a check suddenly showed up for the full tuition. It was a gift from my father's cardiology friend. I asked how I could possibly repay such kindness, and he simply said, 'Whenever you have a chance to help someone in need, do it. It will always come back to you.' His words became the guiding principle of my life."

When I asked what she would want people to say about her, she said, "I hope they say that I was the best possible parent to my son and that the world is better for my son being in it." I know the world is better for Dr. Leyva being in it.

Luis Manrique, MD

Dr. Manrique is an internist with a specialty in infectious diseases. He attended medical school in his home country of Peru at Cayetano Heredia University, where college and medical school were combined into an eight-year program. He came to the United States for his residency in internal medicine at Chicago's Cook County Hospital, and then fellowship in infectious diseases at Rush-Presbyterian St. Luke's Hospital in Chicago.

When he made the decision to go into medicine at the age of thirteen, Dr. Manrique knew he would have an uphill battle. Admission to medical school was determined solely by the score on one college entrance test. He would be competing with twenty-five hundred other applicants for just forty positions. But his determination and study were rewarded by a high score on the entrance test, and he became one of the forty elite. He did equally well in medical school, and, after graduation, he was required to practice for a year in his home country.

He was assigned to work in the jungles of the Amazon, where he moved from village to village with nurses and set up a tent for his "traveling salvation show." Little testing was available, and he had to make most of his diagnostic decisions based on the patient's history and physical exam only. After he completed his required twelve months, he emigrated to the United States, where he would have the opportunity to use sophisticated diagnostics like CT and MRI that either did not exist or were severely restricted in Peru.

He applied for a residency in internal medicine at Cook County Hospital in Chicago. The day before the interview, his bus (the only transportation he could afford) was stuck in a major snowstorm somewhere between his sister's house in New Jersey and his destination, Chicago. He traveled intermittently through the night whenever the roads were opened and arrived just hours before his morning interview. Like many struggling doctors in training, he turned his trial into triumph. The admissions committee was so impressed with his credentials and his determination to make the interview that they offered him the position.

Unfortunately, at the time the practice of medicine at Cook County Hospital was only marginally better than in the Amazon, with large wards of sick patients separated only by cardboard partitions. He did, however, have access to the sophisticated testing that he lacked in his home country, but the bad news was he had to do it himself—draw his own blood, perform most procedures, and transport his patients to radiology, since there were few technicians. Nevertheless, like everything he attempted, he excelled and ultimately earned a position as a fellow in his chosen specialty of infectious diseases at a prestigious Chicago medical center.

Now in private practice, he has become one of my main consultants in infectious diseases, although I think he has given up drawing his own blood and transporting patients to X-ray.

Thomas Marshall, MD

Dr. Marshall is a general internist who practiced in Wheaton, Illinois, for over thirty years until his recent retirement. He attended medical school at the University of Kansas and completed his residency in internal medicine at St. Luke's Hospital in Kansas City, Missouri. Although he moved to Philadelphia for an infectious disease fellowship, he never actually enrolled in the program.

"In retrospect, I'm so glad that happened. I have been much more satisfied as a general internist," he told me. He worked for two years in Philadelphia as an emergency physician until his brother, who was serving a mission in Taiwan, encouraged him to do the same. Within weeks, Dr. Marshall accepted the challenge and uprooted his growing family for a two-year mission to Taiwan. There he supervised medical residents and gained notoriety for feeding patients clay. (That's right, clay!)

One night, he received a desperate call from a new resident who had just admitted a patient with an intentional overdose of the herbicide paraquat. That was a compound that was popularly used for suicide, since the ingestion of even small doses was universally fatal. Dr. Marshall was familiar with the use of activated charcoal to absorb many toxic chemicals, but this was not available in their poor Taiwanese hospital. They knew that paraquat was inactivated by contact with dirt, so they wondered if kaolin, a clay-based product used for diarrhea, would do the same thing.

"We have nothing to lose," said Dr. Marshall to his panicked resident. "Let's try it."

When their patient survived, news of their radical treatment spread throughout the entire country, and Dr. Marshall was featured as a hero on Taiwan television. This treatment soon became the standard of care for every intentional or accidental ingestion of the popular herbicide, reducing the death rate from nearly 100 percent to 30 percent.

I asked Dr. Marshall for his motivation to enter medical school and was expecting to hear some deeply moving story, but he surprised me when he said, "At the time the Vietnam War was in full swing, and I had my choice of killing or saving. I chose saving."

Dr. Marshall and I started internal medicine practices in our small community-based hospital at about the same time. I miss his passionate advocacy for his patients and for patient care in general. Slowing down in retirement is not in his nature, and he is already planning the first of many humanitarian trips.

His answer to my question of what he would want others to know about his life was simple. "I want my epitaph to say, 'He loved life, he loved the Lord, and he loved his family.'"

John P. Mendenhall, MD

Dr. Mendenhall is now retired after a successful forty-year practice of general orthopedic surgery. He graduated from the University of Utah Medical School and practiced in Ogden, Utah.

When I asked him how he became interested in orthopedics, he told me that when he was looking at different surgical specialties, he spent a day with a local orthopedic surgeon. "The morning started out with surgery, using my hands with the type of carpentry tools I love. Then in the afternoon, there were no cases, so we went fishing. I knew then that this was the specialty for me!"

In retirement, he continues to work with carpentry tools and has a business that intentionally loses money. "I just like to help people," he told me. He gets regular calls from neighbors and friends who need his carpentry skills for a leaky roof, a flooded basement, a new shower, and other repairs that the family cannot afford. He sometimes even gets paid.

He continues to be physically active at the age of seventy-seven and annually runs a marathon, except for one year when he hiked and canoed around the Arctic Circle.

John J. Messitt, MD

Dr. Messitt's specialty is obstetrics and gynecology and general endocrinology, an interesting and unusual combination. He graduated from Loyola University Medical School, and, after a residency in obstetrics and gynecology, he did an extra fellowship at Loyola in general endocrinology. Until his retirement in 2014, he practiced in Wheaton, Illinois, and was on the faculty of Northwestern University, and then Loyola University.

He is an Eagle Scout and one of the first to participate in the premier scout camp in New Mexico, Philmont.

When I asked about his career, he replied, "I loved the practice of medicine. I was the luckiest guy in the world."

However, when I asked about his greatest accomplishment in life he replied, "I have six children, all with master's degrees, and no one is in debt."

"What do you mean?" I asked.

"They made it through school without student or other loans," he said. "That's why I'm not driving a Mercedes."

David Mochel, MD

Dr. Mochel is a highly successful orthopedic surgeon with a specialty of total joint surgery. He trained at the University of Illinois College of Medicine and has a busy practice in Wheaton, Illinois. He has personally replaced both knees and both hips on one of my family members (and she is still walking).

He is a devout family man, and that includes the family pets. In fact, the day before a major downstate golf championship for his son, the beloved family dog, Gray, dropped over in the kitchen from a cardiac arrest. Everyone was so upset that Dr. Mochel did CPR on the dog until he was revived. Unfortunately, after a visit to the emergency veterinarian late that night, they learned that the dog could not survive much longer and would need to be put down. "That was the first time—and the last time—I will ever do CPR on an animal," he told me.

Dr. Mochel regularly attends church with his family and believes that his story about the out-of-body experience of his patient, Mary, has no scientific explanation. When he told me the touching story ("Mary's Christmas Carol") I asked who else knew about his experience. "No one but family members," he replied. "I'd be afraid to tell anyone else."

Robin Mraz, MD

Dr. Mraz has been an emergency department physician for fifteen years at Northwestern Medicine Central DuPage Hospital, a Chicago suburban hospital. She excels in a predominantly male specialty and loves the often frenetic pace in the emergency department. She received her medical degree from the University of Illinois College of Medicine and completed her residency in emergency medicine at Advocate Christ Medical Center in Oak Lawn, Illinois.

Like many of the physicians I interviewed, she was the first person in her family to attend college. "What kept you on track?" I asked her.

"I think my boyfriend's family had something to do with it. I started dating John at age fifteen, and we ultimately married and now have three wonderful children. His family expected him to go to college, and they encouraged me to take the same path."

In response to my standard question of what she considered her major accomplishment, she replied simply, "Mom."

"To me, that means raising kids who do the right thing when no one asks them. I would like to think that we taught our kids by example, to do things quietly, not looking for accolades. That's how we should all live our lives. My job in the ED is hard work and stressful and frequently thankless, and if people understood that, they would have a different perspective on what is important," she said.

"What is important to you?" I asked.

"Family, health, teachers, and faith. There are things that happen to me and others almost daily that would not happen if there were not a higher power. I am thankful to know that and to have been given the opportunity, through my patient, Cleveland Manning (chapter three), to listen to the music of heaven."

Kevin Russeau, DC

Dr. Russeau is a chiropractic physician in private practice in Wheaton, Illinois. He earned his degree from Palmer College of Chiropractic in 1992 and has continued his education, earning degrees in neurology, forensics, and consulting.

Dr. Russeau told me that he first fell in love with his profession when he took a job in high school cleaning a chiropractic office after school. He loved to hear stories of how patients got relief from their musculoskeletal pain. His present practice not only includes direct patient care but also consulting for local authorities and other healthcare providers.

His lifelong hobby is photography, and he admits to carrying a camera with him everywhere. On a trip to Yellowstone National Park, he set up his tripod on the street hoping to capture a nearby grizzly. Fortunately, a passing ranger realized he was dangerously close and intercepted him before he obtained a close-up of grizzly tonsils.

Dr. Russeau's story of being miraculously guided to help a depressed patient considering suicide (chapter nineteen) has strengthened his belief that we really are influenced by the Master Healer.

John M. Saran, MD

Dr. Saran is a general internist in private practice for over thirty years in Naperville, Illinois. He graduated from Loyola University Stritch School of Medicine in Maywood, Illinois, where he completed his residency and served as chief resident.

As the oldest of eight children, he was frequently called upon to help with the care of his younger siblings. He not only accepted this responsibility but relished the opportunity to serve. "I think this started my lifelong mission to serve and teach. The practice of medicine is just an extension of that mission," he told me.

One of his great loves is fishing. I asked him to tell me a fishing story that was at least partially true, and, without hesitation and with a twinkle in his eye, he related this spectacular adventure that took place in the waters around a Pacific island. He chartered a boat from an unusually young and inexperienced captain. When they pulled out of the harbor, all the boats went to the right, and his was the only boat that went to the left. "This is where the best fishing is," explained the captain. And he was right. They caught some large fish, until their boat was rocked by explosions coming from a nearby island. He soon learned that they were fishing in restricted waters around an island used on rare occasions for target practice. This happened to be one of those rare occasions.

"It was like the movie *Saving Private Ryan*," Dr. Saran told me, "with the high-pitched whistling of shells going right overhead. I had visions of the headlines in our Chicago newspapers, 'Naperville Physician Killed in Pacific War Games.'" Fortunately they sped away without injury or arrest.

Dr. Saran is a member of the prestigious Alpha Omega Alpha Honor Medical Society, and, for his outstanding teaching to physician assistants at Midwestern University (his other love and mission), he was awarded "Teacher of the Year."

John Showalter, MD

Dr. Showalter is now retired from a distinguished career as an orthopedic surgeon with a specialty in hand surgery. He graduated from Loyola Stritch School of Medicine, served a surgical residency at the University of Iowa, and completed his training in orthopedics at Indiana University and the Indiana Hand Center in Indianapolis.

He told me that he wanted to do his orthopedic training at the University of Iowa but was not accepted. That was a tremendous disappointment at the time, but what he discovered at Indiana was his true love, hand surgery, combined with the new specialty of microsurgery. Had he been at the University of Iowa, he would never have been exposed to microsurgery, since it was only offered at a handful of training centers in the country. Microsurgery (operating with a microscope to reattach tiny blood vessels and nerves) would ultimately become a major part of his practice and the source of his outstanding reputation.

His Indiana training allowed him to perform the first hand reattachment in the Chicagoland area. The year was 1978, and he had been anticipating the procedure, but few surgeons in the world had actually reattached a severed hand. He received the fateful call from a doctor at a local Chicagoland emergency room who had heard about Dr. Showalter. The patient was a young man who had just run a power saw through his forearm.

"Put the hand on ice and send the ambulance right here," he said, his adrenalin pumping. His next call was to the operating room, where he activated the team that had been practicing for just such an emergency. Within a few minutes, the young man arrived and was whisked off to the OR. Now it was up to him. This was the opportunity he was anticipating, the opportunity to use his microsurgical training for something he had never done before. The entire hospital was abuzz with excitement. Every few minutes, a hospital employee or physician peeked into the room to witness history being made. The procedure involved meticulously reattaching each vein, artery, nerve, muscle, and bone. It turned out to be a fourteen-hour procedure that required two separate operating room teams and boxes and boxes of pizza that were generously supplied by the hospital for the inevitable food breaks during such a long surgery.

"Were you exhausted?" I asked Dr. Showalter.

"Not a bit," he told me. "I was so pumped, I never realized it took as long as it did." When he finished, he slept in the hospital so he could check the hand every few hours. As the long night faded into the day, the hand remained pink, and he realized his experiment was a success. The young man went on to live a normal life in every way. His only complaint was that when he played football and caught a pass, his hand sometimes tingled.

Dr. Showalter's experience of being rejected by Iowa seems to be the story of his life. "I am grateful for the opportunities that have arisen out of disappointments," he told me. "Everything is providential, especially those things that we think we know best."

Dr. Showalter's life is also one of giving back. I have known him for thirty years and until his interview, never knew the extent of his service. Every week for over twenty years, he traveled to a local youth prison for an evening of prayer and devotionals for the young inmates. He and his wife participate in CASA, an advocacy organization for at-risk children, and he serves meals under the PADS program to the homeless.

When I finished his interview, I was reminded of the Jimmy Stewart classic that so epitomizes Dr. Showalter's accomplishments, *It's a Wonderful Life.*

Noemi Sigalove, MD

Dr. Sigalove is a general surgeon in private practice in Wheaton, Illinois. She graduated from Rush Medical College and served her residency in general surgery at Rush-Presbyterian St. Luke's Medical Center in Chicago, Illinois. When she was training in the nineties, it was rare for a woman to enter a general surgical specialty. Out of a class of twenty-eight residents, she was the only female. Her nickname with the attending physicians was "The Girl." In fact, when she first announced her intention to go into surgery during her third year in medical school, everyone tried to convince her to enter any other specialty. Even faculty members told her it would be too hard for a woman. Her friends were equally discouraging.

"I'm glad I didn't listen to them," she told me. "Surgery was the only thing I really loved, but they were right about the residency. It was hard, and the surgical mentality was that 'you don't cry.' It hardened me, and I became more like Teflon, but there were times when things didn't bounce off, and I just broke down and wanted to quit." She told me about taking care of a sixteen-year-old boy who came from the Chicago ghetto, where he was shot in the femoral artery in his leg. She took care of him for three months, including his extensive rehab, grew to understand his challenges, and loved him. Then, the day he was released, he was shot in the head by a rival gang member and killed. Upon hearing the news, she broke down and sobbed.

Dr. Sigalove's childhood was no less challenging. She grew up in what is now the Transylvania region of Romania. It was during the Cold War, and her parents refused to join the Communist Party. "Lots of people in our neighborhood just disappeared and were never seen again, and there were many 'suicides' where people mysteriously fell off buildings." Whenever her father was late coming home from work, she feared she would never see him again.

Her parents longed to come to the land of the Statue of Liberty, but they were not allowed to leave Romania. One day, however, they secured a visa to visit Hungary, but they had to leave Noemi and her little sister behind as insurance. From Hungary they were able to escape to Austria, and then to the United States. Dr. Sigalove learned the details when her grandmother, under a veil of secrecy, sped to her home with a truck and packed everything they owned and relocated to a city where they would be unknown. It was a time of great danger and was frightening for a thirteen-year-old girl and her three-year-old sister. The secret police soon found their new location, and, dressed in black, they trailed Noemi to and from school, "Just like in the movies."

After a year of dark uncertainty, a treaty was signed with the United States, granting a loan to Romania. One of the terms was that all the children left behind in Romania had to be released. Noemi finally saw her Statue of Liberty. But that was not the end of her problems. She was a foreigner who did not speak English in a junior high school. With only two outfits to wear and no bra, she was teased to tears and called a communist. With sheer determination, she again overcame adversity and, by high school, was at the top of her class.

Dr. Sigalove ultimately returned to visit her home in Transylvania, but it took thirty years to overcome a fear that she would be trapped again. I asked what she would want others to know about her and she said, "I value independence and freedom, and I love caring for people. One of the best things about being a doctor is it gives you the ability to always do the right thing."

And she does.

HOW THIS BOOK WAS WRITTEN

~

EVERYTHING IN THIS BOOK IS true. It required three years and over two hundred physician interviews to collect a series of stories that satisfied my criteria for inclusion; they had to bring me to tears or give me goose bumps. I wanted to explain exactly how they were written so there would be no question about their authenticity.

Several physicians came to me with stories, but I found many of them by asking around. Most of the doctors came from my hospital, Central DuPage Hospital in Winfield, Illinois, now called Northwestern Medicine after a merger with Northwestern University in Chicago. I have worked with most of these doctors and some for over thirty years.

When I approached physicians, I asked if they had stories of some experiences that they could not explain medically. I quickly learned that most didn't know what I wanted, so, after the introduction, I related a story that I had already collected. Sometimes the telling caused both of us to become emotional. That's when I knew they understood. Some would say that they could not recall any miraculous experience but would think about it. I never heard back from any of those physicians. It was interesting that the doctors who had stories knew immediately. Some were initially hesitant to tell me, but after hearing my story first, they usually lowered their guards.

The most moving experiences were often told in the hospital physicians' lounge, where there is free food and coffee. (I wonder if a full stomach had anything to do with it.) If I recognized a great story, I usually got the basic information, and then asked for a phone number, and, either later that evening or some evening that week, I called the physician directly. I armed myself with several pads of yellow lined paper and about four sharpened pencils. Physicians are a busy bunch. It would not be unusual to call several nights before I was able to connect with the doctor. Sometimes it took weeks. When I made an appointment for an evening phone call, I was more likely to connect.

I sat at my desk, listening to the story and writing as fast as I could. My office staff would say that my handwriting is not the greatest in the first place, and, when I wrote rapidly, it became even worse. However, since I knew the story, I always seemed to be able to decipher my notes. After the doctors finished the stories, and, sometimes during the telling, I asked pertinent questions. This process generally took over an hour. I then obtained additional information on their backgrounds, including education, medical specialty, honors received, and so on. I often asked what they would like me to include in their biographies and what they wanted others to know about their lives. Many times, I knew the physician so well that I already knew a touching life story.

After transcribing the story on multiple sheets of yellow paper, I started typing on my laptop. I am quite accomplished at keyboarding and sometimes joke with my patients that if this doctoring business doesn't work out, I could go into secretarial work. When the story was put down on paper, there were always items that needed further explanation, so, when I finished the first draft, I went through the same process of calling the doctor to review and fill in the gaps. This process was repeated as many as six or seven times for some, but I found that I could usually get the story down in three interactions.

When the story was completed, I usually e-mailed or handed a copy to the doctor, and then scheduled a time when I could go over it with them. At those sessions, we reviewed each word to make sure it was absolutely correct. One of my frequent expressions was, "This story is so spectacular, we don't need any exaggeration." By this session, most of the stories were complete, with only minor changes.

Some of the events the doctors reported happened within the last few weeks or months, but the majority of stories were over a year old, and one happened over thirty years ago. In those cases, the exact words of the conversation were difficult to remember exactly, but the quotations used in the story were as accurate as the physician's memory allowed. In all cases, the words captured the feelings and intent of the conversation. There were also times when a particular item could not be remembered. For example, the color of the car or the temperature outside. In those cases, the physicians made their best guesses. In no case did those little details detract from the meaning of the story.

When the story involved a patient with what may be some sensitive information, the patient was also contacted for permission. Many of the names were changed to protect patient privacy, but the story was not altered. Other times, the location was changed, again to protect the privacy of the patient. Only one physician declined to be acknowledged, and I listed this person as anonymous.

My first editor was always my wife, Joan. She often brought me back to reality. The stories then went to my professional editor, who occasionally modified the sentence structure to change some of my writing from "doctor speak" to real English. Again, the changes only clarified the story and did not alter it.

After the editing, I brought the manuscript back to the physicians to review one last time. If there were no changes, they signed off, and the stories were complete.

Scott J. Kolbaba, MD

Acknowledgments

~

First I would like to acknowledge the physicians who were courageous enough and willing to share experiences that many had never revealed before. I know that your stories will help countless people find peace in what can be a troubling life.

I am also incredibly thankful for the mentoring and encouragement of Scott Macdonald. He was the first person to recognize how moving these stories could be and what an impact they would have on readers. Thank you for keeping me on track and always believing in me.

I am also indebted to my very patient wife, Joan, for putting up with my absence as I was compiling this book and for her exceptional editing and encouragement. She reviewed every story and frequently commented, "This is not good enough; you can do better." Then five or six revisions later, if I saw a smile or a tear, and sometimes both, I knew I had captured the true essence of the doctor's experience.

I also want to thank my accomplished editor who worked tirelessly to help complete the review of my manuscript with all the required deadlines.

My son, Florin, should also be acknowledged for naming the book.

Dane, who enjoys telling me that he is my "firstborn son" was also instrumental in all aspects of the marketing.

I've Had an Experience Like That Too!

~

If you have an "untold story," I'd be delighted to consider it for my next book or for my website. Your miraculous experience may inspire countless others around the world. Simply send a summary of your experience or a full telling of your story to the mailing address or website listed below. No medical degree required.

Scott J. Kolbaba, MD
Untold Stories
P.O. Box 4407
Wheaton, IL 60189

PhysiciansUntoldStories.com

Made in the USA
San Bernardino, CA
25 April 2018